Unofficial "Half-Blood Prince™" Update

W. Frederick Zimmerman, NIMBLE BOOKS

Full review and analysis of everything known so far about book six in the Harry Potter series by J.K. Rowling: HARRY POTTER AND THE HALF-BLOOD PRINCE™.

NIMBLE BOOKS

ISBN: 0-9754479-3-9

Library of Congress Pre-assigned Control Number (PCN): 2004096646

Copyright 2004 W. Frederick Zimmerman d/b/a Nimble Books.

Version 1.0, last saved **2004-09-30.**

Table of Contents

Readers and reviewers, here's what to expect

This is a work of news reporting and analysis which describes what is currently known and speculated about "Harry Potter and the Half-Blood Prince," book six in the Harry Potter series by J. K. Rowling (henceforth also referred to interchangeably as "Half-Blood Prince" or "HBP"). The reporting and analysis in this book is unofficial, unauthorized, and unconfirmed.

Be aware that there are a lot of quotations in this book! In case you're wondering, *that's a good thing* because it means that you know exactly what the real facts are and you know exactly where they are coming from. That makes this a book that you can trust, and that you can refer to over and over again.

You may also notice that major sections or mini-chapters usually begin on a new page, which often results in the preceding page being rather short. This is deliberate, partly for stylistic reasons, and partly so as to allow frequent updating as new information is released about "Half-Blood Prince."

Understand when this book was written

This book was written before the publication of "Half-Blood Prince." More specifically, this particular version was finished on September 30, 2004. Any new information that was released after that date will not be included here. The book will be updated after HBP is released, with new content including a reader's guide to the published book.

> An unofficial report on Harry Potter Book Seven will be issued by Nimble Books soon after the publication of "HBP."

Read this book if ...

- You, or someone you love, have enjoyed J. K. Rowling's Harry Potter books.

- You want to learn interesting things you may have missed in the Harry Potter books.

- You like challenges. I'm going to try to keep things clear for you, but I'm also going to teach you how to learn about subjects that interest you – and that means reading challenging stuff, just like Harry, Hermione, and Ron have to do at Hogwarts!

Don't bother if ...

- You are totally uninterested in children, young adults, or fantasy fiction. (In other words, if you are a complete and hopeless Muggle!)

Spoiler warning: stop here if ...

- You don't want to encounter spoilers.

A "spoiler" is advance information about a book or movie that would "spoil" the experience of seeing the actual work. Book and movie reviewers generally take care to warn readers of potential spoilers. Internet posters who have advance information that others may not yet have seen usually include the word "SPOILER" in the title of their article, and sometimes add extra lines to their post or otherwise hide their content so that casual readers have additional protection against encountering spoilers.

> This entire book should be considered to have a SPOILER warning affixed. If you really hate getting advance info about books or movies, don't read this book!

Having done my duty and issued a spoiler warning, I can now tell you that there are no *true* spoilers in this book: there are no secrets revealed that would ruin any dramatic surprises in "Harry Potter and the Half-Blood Prince™". Instead, there is a patient, searching accumulation of many details found in the public record. Put together, these details will add much to your understanding and appreciation of the "Harry Potter" series.

Warning: I have no sources of inside information and I have not spoken with or heard from J. K. Rowling, her publishers, her film company, or anyone who is in any way officially connected with the books. The contents of this report are unofficial and unauthorized. Although J. K. Rowling, etc. have not confirmed any of the specific statements in the book, I have taken great care to tell you where I found particular pieces of information. When the source is J. K. Rowling, you can probably count on it! Otherwise, it's speculative.

Understand how this book is organized and what it contains

This book is loosely grouped into five major parts:

- Information specifically about book six, "Harry Potter and the Half-Blood Prince."

- Information that pertains both to book six and to book seven in the series.

- Information specifically related to book seven.

- Information on books by Rowling *beyond* book seven.

- Tips on what to do while you wait!

The Appendix contains the Usenet newsgroup alt.fan.harry-potter's Frequently Asked Questions file (FAQ), which covers issues ranging from book one through book seven.

As research for this book, I read:

- Every on-line chat that J. K. Rowling has ever done.

- More than 250 news articles mentioning the quoted phrase "Half-Blood Prince" in a leading news warehouse and more than 320 articles identified by Google News as mentioning the quoted phrase "Half-Blood Prince."

- 377 blogs mentioning the quoted phrase "Half-Blood Prince" in the blog search engine Feedster.

- More than 1000 articles posted on Usenet newsgroup alt.fan.harry-potter.

- Hundreds of posts on dozens of Potter-related websites.

- Dozens of trademark applications at the UK and US patent offices.

- Numerous biographies and critical works about J. K. Rowling.
- And, of course, the entire series to date!

This book contains the results of my research. Over the years and especially in recent months, J. K. Rowling and others have let slip quite a bit of information about "Harry Potter and the Half-Blood Prince." I think I was able to pull together a lot of interesting information. You will notice that there are many quotations and that wherever possible I have provided an "attribution"—that is, I have identified author, title, date, and place of publication (often Internet). That way, you can judge for yourself whether my sources are solid. ✗

About the author

W. Frederick Zimmerman is the publisher of Nimble Books. He is also a Research Scientist for ISciences, L.L.C, an information sciences consulting firm located in Ann Arbor, Michigan. He earned a B.A. with Honors from Swarthmore College and a J.D. from Wayne State University. More importantly than any of that, he has read all of the Harry Potter books with his daughter Kelsey. He read the first three to her aloud, before she got too smart for him.

About the illustrator

Jana Pokorny says:

> "I was born in 1982 in Berlin, Germany. Right now I'm a student. I draw since I can remember. I started to draw Harry Potter stuff right after I've seen the first movie. I really love Harry Potter and that's my way to show it. I don't have a professional education, it's just talent but I'm still learning. More under http://www.soulsembrace.de." ✎

About Nimble Books

Our trusty Merriam-Webster Collegiate Dictionary defines "nimble" as follows:

> 1: quick and light in motion: AGILE *nimble fingers*
>
> 2 a: marked by quick, alert, clever conception, comprehension, or resourcefulness *a nimble mind* b: RESPONSIVE, SENSITIVE *a nimble listener*

And traces the etymology to the 14th Century:

> Middle English nimel, from Old English numol holding much, from niman to take; akin to Old High German neman to take, Greek nemein to distribute, manage, nomos pasture, nomos usage, custom, law

The etymology is reminiscent of the old Biblical adage, "to whom much is given, much is expected" (Luke 12:48). Nimble Books seeks to honor that Christian principle by combining the spirit of *nimbleness* with the Biblical concept of *abundance:* we deliver what you need to know about a subject in a quick, resourceful, and sensitive manner. ✗

Acknowledgements

First, last, and always, my lovely wife, Cheryl.

Our wonderful daughter Kelsey.

Our wonderful son Parker, who may just grow up to be a Harry Potter fan.

Harry Potter fans everywhere, who shared so much useful information with each other and with me.

The great people on alt.fan.harry-potter (AFHP), including Troels Forchhammer.

Cooper Lewis.

Clarimonde at the Sugar Quill.

Petrea Mitchell, author of the alt.fan.harry-potter FAQ.

Hilary Gowen.

"The Q Engima."

Bethbethbeth.

Racheline Maltese.

And, of course, J. K. Rowling, for giving the world these books that reflect love, intelligence, generosity and courage. ✗

How to pronounce "Rowling"

Stephen Fry is an English actor who is the narrator of the Harry Potter audio books. In an interview in 2003 he cleared up a crucial issue.

> Stephen Fry: Can we settle a really important question? How do you pronounce your last name?

> JK Rowling: It is Rowling – as in rolling pin.

> Stephen Fry: Rolling! You now all have to say after me, the word "rolling" boys and girls, 1...2...3...

> Audience: ROLLING!

> Stephen Fry: If you hear anybody in the future say JK "Row-elling" you have my permission to hit them on the head - not with a copy of the Order of the Phoenix because that would be cruel

> JK Rowling: That would kill them :o)

> Stephen Fry: No use something smaller than the last book— like a fridge. JK Rowling (laughs) (MSN UK, 6/26/03, http://www.msn.co.uk/liveevents/harrypotter/transcript/Default.asp?Ath=f) ✎

Christianity and Harry Potter

The Harry Potter phenomenon has sparked a great deal of controversy among Christians. Obviously, my own view is that the Potter books are good for children; but as a Christian, I feel a responsibility to acknowledge and address the issues before encouraging readers to plunge into this book.

The fundamental issues

One fundamental problem is that the Bible is full of very clear commands forbidding the practice of witchcraft, while the Harry Potter books are full of elaborate descriptions of witchcraft and wizardry. See, for example, Deuteronomy 18:10:

> Let no one be found among you who sacrifices his son or daughter in [or who makes his son or daughter pass through] the fire, who practices divination or sorcery, interprets omens, engages in witchcraft ... [NIV]

Another fundamental problem is that the Bible is full of very clear commands that members of the Body of Christ should spend their time on loving Christ and following the Bible, whereas the Bible is not at all full of commands that we should spend our time reading children's books and novels.

Rowling's own views

J. K. Rowling has been close-mouthed about her own religious faith. Here is the most candid personal statement I was able to find.

> **E:** But in your own life, I mean, are you a churchgoer?
>
> **JK:** (Nods) Mmm hmm. Well I go more than to weddings and christenings. Yes, I do.
>
> **E:** And in your own life, would the church and that kind of spirituality help you deal with the loss of your mum?
>
> **JK:** No, actually it didn't at the time. No. (Shakes her head)
>
> **E:** So you've come back to it.
>
> **JK:** Yeah, I would say so. I have some problems with conventional organized religion. Some problems. (Long pause) But...but, yes, it's a place I would go to in a time of trouble. It probably is a place I would go to in a time of trouble. I wouldn't expect it to provide all the answers, 'cause I would expect to find some of those within me.

E: Right, but the institutional side of it, you know, the rules…

JK: I have certain problems with some aspects of that. Yes I do. (CBC Hot Type interview, 7/13/00, http://www.cbc.ca/hottype/season99-00/00-06-23_interview.html)

I might mention here that quite a few important Christians, such as Martin Luther, John Wesley, and, hey, *just about every other Protestant alive since 1519,* have some problems with certain aspects of organized religion.

In the spirit of fairness, it is clear that J. K. Rowling may have some Christian sympathies and feelings, but she is not a practicing, committed, believing Christian. The question is, does that mean we should shut the door on her books?

What I Believe

It seems clear to me, having read all her books and every published interview that I could find, that J. K. Rowling does not intend for children to throw themselves into the practice of witchcraft.

It also seems clear to me that Christ did not intend that Christians should only enjoy works of art produced by practicing Christians.

The word Christians use is "discernment." We must be careful to discern the true meaning and true implications of what we read. With that in mind, here's my bottom line.

I believe that J. K. Rowling's agenda is to tell a cracking good story that encourages children to make good choices. When you read, remember that this is a pretend story, and remember that the Bible tells us to be very careful about witchcraft and wizardry, and focus on what J. K. Rowling is trying to tell us about goodness and love.

As the Gospels say,

> "where your treasure is, there your heart will be also." (NIV, Matthew 6:21, Luke 12:34).

And Jesus told us:

> 'Love the Lord your God with all your heart and with all your soul and with all your mind. This is the first and greatest commandment. And the second is like it: 'Love your neighbor as yourself.' (NIV, Matthew 22:37-39).

When you read J. K. Rowling's books, let it be for the glory of God. ✎

Part One: Harry Potter book six—
"Harry Potter and the Half-Blood Prince"

When will "Half-Blood Prince" be released??

As soon as it's done. Don't worry, even though J. K. Rowling's pregnant for the third time, she still plans to finish the book.

> "Let me reassure you that book six remains well on track and, fingers crossed of course, I don't foresee any baby-related interruptions or delays," Rowling said. "I still can't say for sure when it will be finished, but I have written a lot and I really like it." (AP, August 2, 2004).

Why "Lemony Snicket Fans" are happier than "Harry Potter" fans

A married couple on LiveJournal laid down a funny riff about how long it takes J. K. Rowling to write a new book.

altoidsaddict: Hey! The Grim Grotto comes out soon!

hpsf_phoenix: Oh, yeah? Well, the new Harry Potter... the... it... you're dumb.

altoidsaddict: At least I have a fandom where the author actually *produces* instead of being all "Crumpets! Oooh! Pillars of Storgé! Tea! Mummy! Half-Blood Prince! Something! Off to have a baby now!" http://www.livejournal.com/users/altoidsaddict/206943.html

Ok, but really, when will it be done?

When J. K. Rowling's publishers, Bloomsbury (U.K.) and Scholastic (U.S.), announce the release date, it will be worldwide news. Just keep an eye on CNN.

Measuring JKR's progress

As of March 15, 2004, she wrote:

> Book six is well underway, hooray, though I am still at the stage where I have a large and complicated chart propped on the desk in front of me to remind me what happens where, how, to whom and which bits of crucial information need to be slipped into which innocent-looking chapters.

> I started writing Harry Potter Six before my son David (who has just turned one) was born, but then took a bit of a break during the serious sleep-deprivation phase of his babyhood. (jkrowling.com, http://www.jkrowling.com/textonly/news_view.cfm?id=62)

On July 24, 2004 she described the book's status this way:

> So let me reassure you that book six remains well on track and, fingers crossed of course, I don't foresee any baby-related interruptions or delays. I still can't say for sure when it will be finished, but I have written a lot and I really like it (a reckless challenge to fate, that; I bet the next chapter goes horribly wrong now).

So clearly it was not finished as of July 24.

How can I know when it is released for sure?

You can sign up for e-mail notification of the release of "Harry Potter and the Half-Blood Prince" at Amazon.com and Barnesandnoble.com. Just do a search on "Half-Blood Prince" and look for the e-mail signup box.

Tip: it may just be easier to keep an eye on your local bookstore. It's exciting to pre-order at one of the online retailers, but you wind up waiting longer for the book than you would if you just go to the bookstore at midnight the day the book is released.

Who will be the first to learn the Half-Blood Prince's identity?

Smart money is on Rowling's daughter, Jessica. Rowling commented on her website in July 2004: "Jessica loves the books, which is very nice of her as she's had to share me with Harry for so long." ✗

How we know the title

J. K. Rowling released it on her web site on a page that looked like this:

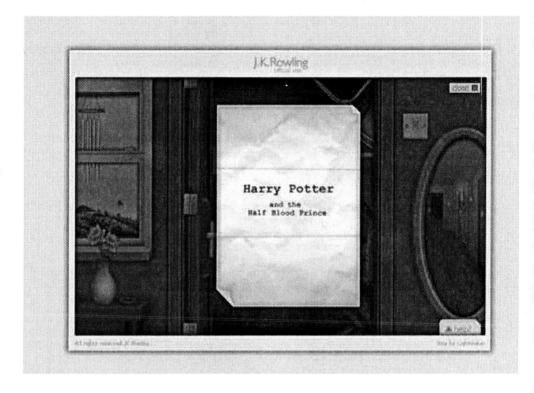

Figure 1. The title of book six, from jkrowling.com.

She confirmed that it was the genuine title in this message on her web site.

> Well, the door opened at last and I showed you the title of book six - the genuine title, the title that will appear on the published book, the title I have been using in my head for ages and age ...

> Information you take directly from this site will be truthful and accurate (I might occasionally joke, but as time goes on, you'll learn to tell when I'm joking). Do not trust anybody else claiming to have found information on this site that you cannot access, however seemingly convincing the images they provide to support their story.

> I never post information on the site that I do not want fans to read immediately. In other words, anybody claiming to have 'discovered' a message that wasn't due for release yet is lying.

This last bit referred to a hoax title that had been released a few days earlier. The hoax title will be discussed later in this Part of the book so as not to confuse you with wrong information right at the beginning.

Maybe this whole spoiler thing isn't that important anyway?

Before we go too much further with the "Half-Blood Prince" investigation, maybe we should pause for a moment's reflection about the whole idea of getting advance information ("spoilers") about forthcoming books. Livejournal poster Ursa Major laid down a nice rant on the subject.

> a question about spoilers: when has it gone too far? and i mean this in the broadest sense possible. For example, it was front-page news on CNN this morning that the title for the new harry potter book is **harry potter and the half-blood prince**.
>
> i have two questions:
>
> 1. how does that warrant front-page news on CNN?
>
> 2. how does the mere *title* of an upcoming (and as-of-yet not fully written!) book warrant [editing out spoilers]? because, honestly? said book is not going to be released for at least a year, if not more. and yet, several people on my friends list [at Live Journal] are *afraid* to actually say what the title is, despite JK Rowling broadcasting it for public release on her own website, for fear of being jumped on by the spoiler-hypochondriacs. "help! you told me what the title was! ... i am now *contaminated!* you've ruined the book for meeee!!!" ...so, when is it reasonable to expect to be able to talk freely about a given event/story? does it matter if it's fictional or real? does it vary between media? ...
>
> i'm the kind of person who decides whether or not she wants to buy a book based on reading the last chapter, not the first. i'm impatient. :) but i realize not everyone else feels this way, so i lj-cut for major plot points and actual dialogue excerpts. if it's been in a commercial or in any sort of official promotion, though, for the most part, i feel it's fair game. what do you think? (http://www.livejournal.com/users/ursamajor/383236.html) [warning: web-site uses some "R" language].

My basic answer to this is yes, right, absolutely, you're making good sense!

On ursamajor's first point, it *is* somewhat ridiculous to get this excited about the title of a book before it's even out ... but the fact that you're reading this book tells me that you're one of those people, like me, who does get excited about stuff like that! That's life, people get excited about things.

On ursamajor's second point, obviously, I completely agree … if it's been published publicly, it's fair game. If you don't want to read advance information, then don't click on the links when you see them!

Maybe the whole "Half-Blood Prince" thing isn't really that important anyway?

Ok, so we've decided that we do care about Harry Potter book six. But maybe the title's not so important, eh? Shortly after the title was released, one Usenet poster, Toon, floated the idea that the title wasn't very important.

> Going by the last two titles, HBP is pretty much a minor occurrence.

> Goblet Of Fire is barely used, except to get Harry into the Tournament.

Smaug69 shot this down rather easily.

> LOL. It was only the manner in which Voldemort was able to get Harry away from Hogwart's and Dumbledore so he could carry out his plan. It set everything in motion. It's not the quantity, it's the quality.

> > The Order, although important overall series wise, had little to do with the book.

> What book were you reading? The Order of the Phoenix was prominently used in the HP&OotP.

> > So, I'm thinking the HBP will be some guy who shows up, and maybe one of his > entourage is key, or …

> Or he'll play as pivotal a role as the Philosopher's Stone, Chamber of Secrets, Prisoner of Azkaban, Goblet of Fire and Order of the Phoenix have done in their respective books. (alt.fan.harry-potter, 7/2/04).

In other words, pretty darned pivotal! So let's go on the assumption that "Half-Blood Prince" is an important part of Harry Potter book six, and try to figure out what it means.

WHY "HALF-BLOOD PRINCE" FANS ARE SMARTER THAN "REVENGE OF THE SITH" FANS

"Potter fans spent scant time debating that title's merits before moving on to figure out who the prince will be (Neville's frog? The boy mentioned five times in the second book?) But the notoriously finicky Star Wars fans have spent days arguing about Lucas' [title] selection.

A quick survey of Internet message boards and news stories Monday showed that many fans like it, which already puts it ahead of the last title, Attack of the Clones.

> Of those who don't like it, their gripes include: Lucas just picked a title from the fan rumor mill. This makes too many Star Wars titles with "of the" in them. The Sith don't have anything to revenge, so they should be rising, or returning, or revamping, or re-something elseing. And if this movie is as bad as Clones, it's not smart to give it the acronym ROTS." (Sharon Fink, St. Petersburg Times (Fl.), July 27, 2004).

Confirming it's "Half-Blood Prince" with the hyphen

The well-regarded website The Leaky Cauldron checked on the spelling of 'half-blood prince" and received exclusive confirmation.

> TLC has received official confirmation from Scholastic that the title of the sixth book will be *Harry Potter and the Half-Blood Prince*, with a hyphen connecting "Half" and "Blood," matching the way "half-blood" is spelled in the books. This is the format in which Scholastic will be producing the book. Apologies to all the theorists who were excited about the missing piece of punctuation. :) ... (The Leaky Cauldron, 8/22/04, http://www.the-leaky-cauldron.org/MTarchives/week_2004_08_22.html)

What is a "Half-Blood Prince"?

Let's break it down into two parts, "Half-Blood" and "Prince." "Half-blood" is the compound adjective that modifies the noun, "prince," so let's begin with "prince."

MERRIAM-WEBSTER

According to Merriam-Webster, "prince" has four meanings.

> 1: MONARCH, KING b: the ruler of a principality or state
>
> 2: a male member of a royal family; especially : a son of the sovereign
>
> 3: a nobleman of varying rank and status
>
> 4: one likened to a prince; especially: a man of high rank or of high standing in his class or profession. (Merriam-Webster's 11th Collegiate Dictionary, 2004).

We must assume that J. K. Rowling, as a former Classics major and word-lover, is aware of all these possible meanings, which open up some interesting possibilities.

First, the "historical" meaning, as in a Prince of a German state in the 1600's, or Machiavelli's "The Prince": "the rule of a principality or state." So the "Half-Blood Prince" could be more than just a king-in-waiting—he could be the actual ruler of a different country (probably European).

> For people who like unlikely theories – according to the first dictionary definition of the word, a Prince is simply defined as a "ruler" — which means the "Half-Blood Prince" could be female! Don't bet on it, though.

The second meaning is the most likely: "a male member of a royal family, especially a son of the sovereign." This is thought-provoking because there has been no mention of an English sovereign in the Harry Potter books thus far … but the structure of magic government seems to parallel the contemporary Muggle government in many ways.

Indeed, Muggle England still has Queen Elizabeth II and her son, Charles, the Prince of Wales, who will (probably) become King of Muggle England some day. Charles has two sons from his marriage to the late Princess Diana, and those sons are called Prince William and Prince Harry. (Not that it's crucial, but some princes, like those two, happen to be extremely handsome…)

So, is there a magic royal family, complete with one or more handsome princes? No one knows for sure—yet.

The third meaning of prince is "a nobleman of varying rank and status," a sort of generic aristocrat. It's certainly possible that J. K. Rowling is using the word in this way, but, frankly, for Potter fans, that would be something of a let-down. If he's not a *real* Prince, why use the specific word in the title? I'm betting against this one.

The fourth dictionary meaning of prince is "likened to a prince; especially: a man of high rank or of high standing in his class or profession." The world of J. K. Rowling is already full of people like that … Dumbledore, McGonagall, Voldemort, maybe even Hagrid could fit that description!

(Hagrid? Think about it: gamekeepers all over the world must know how good Hagrid is at raising magical creatures!)

BEYOND MERRIAM-WEBSTER

Tip: never rely on just one dictionary. It's good to consult a few, and to draw on your own experience of how words are used. For example, Usenet poster Dm498@aol.com observed

> First, most are assuming "Prince" refers to royalty. However, 'Prince' could be used figuratively to describe a pampered, spoiled son.

Absolutely true, and the idea of a "prince" as spoiled is one that occurs frequently in fairy tales and common culture. My bet, though, is that J. K. Rowling is too smart and too original to do a remake of "Shrek 2" … so watch for a prince who's neither Charming nor Spoiled!

Another common misconception is that princes must always be young. In fact, this is not the case—England's own current Prince Charles is pushing 50. However, as Usenet poster JayGee observed, there is a literary bias for princes to be young. "Don't gimme any guff about David, Tutankhamen, etc. - you're just confusing historical fact with a perfect potty literary theory)." (alt.fan.harry-potter, 8/19/04).

WHAT'S A "HALF-BLOOD?"

Now that we've looked at the possible meanings of "prince," let's take a look at "half-blood." Firstly, J. K. Rowling did not invent the word "half-blood." It's been around for a while. According to Merriam-Webster, the noun "half blood" (no hyphen) has been around since 1553, and the adjective "half-blood" (with hyphen) since 1605. Secondly, the standard dictionary meaning of the word is different from the way it's used in J. K. Rowling's world.   This might be important.

According to Merriam-Webster, "half blood" means

> the relation between persons having only one parent in common.

In other words, like half-brothers and half-sisters. My half-brother has the same father that I do, but a different mother; or my half-sister has the same mother that I do, but a different father.

The people in J. K. Rowling's world have used the word in a different manner so far. In "Chamber of Secrets," the term "half-blood" is introduced as meaning someone whose ancestry is not "pure-blood"—in other words, a wizard (person with magical powers) who is descended from at least one Muggle. That means most people have at least some half-blood in term. As Ron Weasley says, "If we hadn't married Muggles we'd've have died out!" ("Chamber of Secrets", chapter VII).

If she does mean to use the "magical" meaning of the word, then she's talking about a key character that is a "prince" of some sort and is "half-blood," in other words, with some Muggle in his ancestry.

What if J. K. Rowling does mean to use the common meaning of the word "half-blood"? If she's talking about a key character that has the same father or mother as another character, and is a prince, that's pretty interesting...

Rowling has said on numerous occasions that neither Voldemort nor Harry Potter is the "Half-Blood Prince." (More on this later).

Let's look at the most crucial piece of evidence that we have: the excerpt from HBP that J. K. Rowling published at jkrowling.com in August 2004. ✎

The first known excerpt from HBP

A series of steps on Rowling's web site led the reader to a page that looked like this.

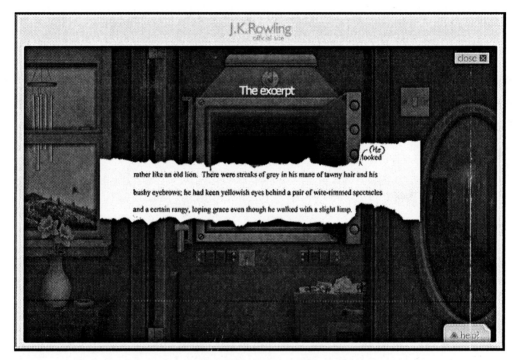

Figure 2. The "tawny-haired" man HBP excerpt at jkrowling.com.

He looked rather like an old lion. There were streaks of grey in his mane of tawny hair and his bushy eyebrows; he had keen yellowish eyes behind a pair of wire-rimmed spectacles and a certain rangy, loping grace even though he walked with a slight limp. (jkrowling.com, 8/20/2004).

Here are the directions that led readers to the picture.

-The door [in Rowling's office] opens to a black room.

-There is a light switch you must click around for, about 1/3 of the way across from the left side of the door, starting from just under the door handle.

A dartboard appears. Use each of the three darts to hit 7, then 1, then 3 (713, the # of the Gringotts vault from SS/PS).

> -A security save appears. The code there is 302723. Much thanks to the Leaky reader "roonwit" who figured this out (the number appears on a business card - for Gobb Lynn Security Systems - that is now tacked to JKR's Extra Stuff section).
>
> The excerpt appears. Enjoy! (The Leaky Cauldron, 8/16/04)

Readers, I'm going to steer you straight. I think this is a description of the "Half-Blood Prince." It's like J. K. Rowling is dropping us a giant hint. First she tells us that the book is going to be called "Harry Potter and the Half-Blood Prince," then she gives us this excerpt. She left other possibilities open, but c'mon, when you look at the facts, this has to be the leading theory. Two plus two equals four.

What if the tawny-haired man is the Half-Blood Prince?

Well, the first thing that jumps out from the excerpt is that he's a good guy. I mean, it doesn't explicitly say so, but it sure sounds like J. K. Rowling wants us to like this guy. She could be doing a massive head-fake and this could be Voldemort's little brother in villainy, but I'm thinking not.

The next thing that jumps out is that he's good-looking. It's usually positive when they say a man looks like a lion, right? (Unless you look like Scar in Disney's "The Lion King.") And "keen, yellowish eyes" and "a certain rangy, loping grace," that's also good stuff for the female contingent. So we know this character is going to be pretty charismatic.

It looks like maybe he's a teacher or some sort of expert—"keen" eyes, "wire-rimmed spectacles."

It sounds like he might be a Quidditch jock—that stuff about a "rangy, loping grace" is similar to the way Harry is described when he's being the Quidditch Seeker.

Also, it sounds like he's about a zillion years old. "Bushy eyebrows," "streaks of grey" in his hair and a limp—sounds like Andy Rooney with a cane! So we're looking at a middle-aged scholar and possible Quidditch jock who's a good-looking nice guy —and a "Half-Blood Prince."

Finally, let's not forget that the full title of the book is "*Harry Potter* and the Half-Blood Prince." This guy is going to be brought into a relationship with Harry, and most likely it will be a positive one, maybe a mentorship.

Who could replace Dumbledore, though? Anyone else would look like a stiff next to the headmaster of Hogwarts. So if the tawny-haired man is going to have a relationship with Harry, either it's going to be some sort of complementary mentor … someone who helps with things that DD doesn't know much about (girls?) or maybe some sort of a rival (but not a downright enemy, for the reasons explained in the first paragraph).

We'll see! ✕

What is the connection between "Chamber of Secrets" and "Half-Blood Prince"?

Now that we've laid out the basic facts about the title, it's time to turn to some important background information that J. K. Rowling has provided. These postings on her web site revealed some crucial information about the relationship of book six to book two in the series.

> I was delighted to see that a hard core of super-bright fans knew that the real title was once, in the long distant past, a possibility for 'Chamber of Secrets', and from that deduced that it was genuine. Certain crucial pieces of information in book six were originally planned for 'Chamber of Secrets', but very early on (first draft of Chamber) I realised that this information's proper home was book six. I have said before now that 'Chamber' holds some very important clues to the ultimate end of the series. Not as many as six, obviously, but there is a link. (jkrowling.com, http://www.jkrowling.com/textonly/news_view.cfm?id=77)

She provided more detail in another article.

> [question] In what way is 'Harry Potter and the Half-Blood Prince' related to 'Harry Potter and the Chamber of Secrets'?

> [answer] I have been engulfed by an avalanche of questions on the subject of 'Prince' having once been a title of 'Chamber'. I am therefore attempting to answer most of them under this heading, which I think just about covers all the answerable variations (the unanswerable ones include questions such as 'who's the Half-Blood Prince?' 'what happens in the Half-Blood Prince?' and 'what does Half-Blood Prince mean?')

> The plot of 'Prince' bears no resemblance whatsoever to the plot of 'Chamber', nor is it an off-cut of 'Chamber'. The story of 'Prince' takes off where 'Phoenix' ended and does not hark back to four years previously. True, mention is made to events that happened in 'Chamber,' but of course, mention is also made of events that happened in 'Stone', 'Azkaban', 'Goblet' and 'Phoenix'.

> 'The Half-Blood Prince' might be described as a strand of the overall plot. That strand could be used in a whole variety of ways and back in 1997 I considered weaving it into the story of 'Chamber'. It really didn't fit there, though; it was not part of the story of the basilisk and Riddle's diary, and before long I accepted that it would be better to do it justice in book six. I clung to the title for a while, even though all trace of the 'Prince' storyline had disappeared, because I liked it so much (yes, I really like this title!). I re-christened book two 'Chamber of Secrets' when I started the second draft. The link I mentioned between books two and six does not, in fact, relate to the 'Half-Blood Prince' (because there is no trace left of the HBP storyline in 'Chamber'.) Rather, it relates to a discovery Harry made in 'Chamber' that foreshadows something that he finds out in 'Prince'. (jkrowling.com, http://www.jkrowling.com/textonly/faq_view.cfm?id=56)

The most important (and frustrating) comment in this essay is that "all trace of the 'Prince' storyline had disappeared." No matter how hard I look at the words in "Chamber of Secrets," they're not going to reveal much about the storyline of HBP, because J. K. Rowling has already specifically gone through and removed those clues! But she does say that "a discovery Harry made in 'Chamber' foreshadows something that he finds out in 'Prince." Notice that Rowling says "a" discovery, not "the discoveries."

Now Harry makes a number of important discoveries in "Chamber of Secrets." Here are a few.

- There is a Chamber of Secrets.
- The back-story of Salazar Slytherin and the founding of Hogwarts.
- Tom Riddle is Voldemort.
- Only a true heir of Godric Gryffindor can pull his sword from the Sorting Hat.
- "It is our choices, Harry, who show us who we really are."

One of these discoveries—or a discovery not listed here—foreshadows a crucial discovery in "Harry Potter and the Half-Blood Prince."

The discovery in HBP has to be something that's big, that relates personally to Harry, and that has not already been discussed to death in previous books. All the other discoveries are old news. Tom Riddle is Lord Voldemort: snore! Salazar Slytherin founded Hogwarts: snoozy snore! My money's on the Godric Gryffindor angle. ✗

Things we will definitely see in book six

I'm going to keep on my theme of giving you the solid information first, so here is some information *specifically relating to book six* that has been confirmed by authoritative sources. Information relating to *either book six or book seven* is discussed in Part Two, and information *relating to book seven alone* is discussed in Part Three. With that in mind, you can count on seeing the following things in book six.

Harry making a short stay at 4 Privet Drive.

> Adele: Will poor Harry be stuck at the Dursleys' all next summer?
>
> JK Rowling replies -> Not all summer, no. In fact, he has the shortest stay in Privet Drive so far. (World Book Day chat, 3/04/04, http://www.mugglenet.com/jkrwbd.shtml).

An update (and probably some major plot action) on Peter Pettigrew.

> Rita: What about Wormtail? Is there hope for redemption?
>
> JK Rowling replies -> There's always hope, of course. You'll find out more about our rat-like friend in book six. (World Book Day chat, 3/04/04, http://www.mugglenet.com/jkrwbd.shtml).

More about Harry's love life, and a little less random anger.

> polly weasley: Will Harry fall for another girl in book six, or will he be too busy for romance?
>
> JK Rowling replies -> He'll be busy, but what's life without a little romance? In book six, the wizarding world is really at war again and he has to master his own feelings to make himself useful. (World Book Day chat, 3/04/04, http://www.mugglenet.com/jkrwbd.shtml).

More about Hagrid's half-brother Grawp.

> Kings Park primary school: What will happen to Hagrid's half brother?
>
> JK Rowling replies -> you'll find out in book six. Luckily he's become a little more controllable. (World Book Day, http://www.mugglenet.com/jkrwbd.shtml ,3/4/04).
>
> Will Hagrid ever succeed with his plans for his brother?
>
> In a limited way, yes. Grawp is obviously the very stupidest thing that Hagrid ever brought home. In his long line of bringing home stupid things—Aragog, the Blast-Ended Skrewts—Grawp is the one that should have finished him off, but ironically it might be the one time that a monstrous something came good. By the next book, Grawp is a little bit more controllable. I think you got a clue to that at

the end of Phoenix, because Grawp was starting to speak and to be a little bit more amenable to human contact. (Edinburgh Book Festival, 8/15/04, http://www.jkrowling.com/textonly/news_view.cfm?id=80) .

More magical activity in Muggledom.

Calliope: Are the Muggle and Magical worlds ever going to be rejoined?

JK Rowling replies -> No, the breach was final, although as book six shows, the Muggles are noticing more and more odd happenings now that Voldemort's back. (World Book Day chat, 3/04/04, http://www.mugglenet.com/jkrwbd.shtml).

More about Voldemort's origins.

mnich: Was Voldemort born evil?

JK Rowling replies -> I don't believe that anybody was born evil. You will find out more about the circumstances of his birth in the next book. (World Book Day chat, 04/04/2004, http://www.mugglenet.com/jkrwbd.shtml).

The Hogwarts Graveyard. (Kudos to the sharp-eyed guys at http://www.halfbloodprince.info for spotting this one, referenced in an interview with "Azkaban" director Alfonso Cuaron.

Question: What was it like meeting JK, what was her advice like?

Alfonso: She [Rowling] said I should stay faithful to the spirit of the book not literal. That was entrusting me a lot of freedom. But freedom and responsibility is the same thing - I was like 'oh gosh - am I being faithful to the spirit?'

The amazing thing with JK as a collaborator is she doesn't stop you doing anything. The way she approaches it has nothing to do with 'I like' or 'I dislike' it's 'this makes sense' or 'it doesn't make sense in this universe.'

I give you an example: There's a scene where Malfoy wants to see Buckbeak being executed. It's where Hermione punches him. And there's a sundial. We thought we need something there. I said 'Let's put a graveyard there'.

She says: 'No, you can't have a graveyard there'. And I'm like, 'Why?' She says: 'Oh because the graveyard is near this other wing of the castle and it's going to play an important part in number six because such and such and such. (CBBC Newsround, 5/28/04,, http://news.bbc.co.uk/cbbcnews/hi/tv_film/newsid_3758000/3758101.stm)

Beware the cliff-hanger!

There is a distinct and frightening possibility that book six will end with an atrocious cliff-hanger. Usenet poster Malachi came up with a good example of the worst-case scenario.

> If you had been reading the Dark Tower series by Stephen King, you probably remember the evil, horrible cliff-hanger he left readers with - for 6 years - between books 3 and 4. If not, here's a summary...
>
> End of book 3 ("The Wastelands") - our heroes are aboard a monorail, hurtling faster than the speed of sound across a blasted, nuclear-wasted land. The monorail is 'run' by an insane artificial intelligence named Blaine ... that has forc[ed] the characters aboard and seal[ed] them in, he has told them that he will be committing suicide by not slowing down at the end of the run - he'll just smash into smithereens.
>
> However, Blaine likes riddles, which the characters are well equipped to dish out, so a deal is made: if the characters can come up with a riddle that Blaine cannot answer, he will spare their lives. Otherwise - ta-ta,bye-bye, don't forget to write, ka-BLAMMO! End of the line.
>
> So the riddling begins.... and there ends book three. 1991.
>
> 1992 - no sequel.
>
> 1993 - no sequel.
>
> 1994, 5, 6...
>
> Readers were going insane. It wasn't until 1997 that book four ("Wizard And Glass") was published. Talk about cruelty! (alt.fan.harry-potter, 7/30/04)

This could happen to us. It's not likely, but it's possible. So be warned! ✒

So who else might be the "Half-Blood Prince"?

As soon as the title was announced, the fan community began buzzing with dozens of theories about the identity of the HBP. As I've said above, the "excerpt" theory is (in my view) the most likely, but it's pretty fun and thought-provoking to look at some of the other theories. First, a rehearsal of the arguments for the leading candidate, the tawny-haired man.

The HBP is the person in the excerpt

Arguments in favor of this possibility:

- Take a hint! J. K. Rowling released the excerpt after she released the title for the book.

- The titles in each of the stories thus far have described new characters or objects, not existing ones with a makeover.

  The pattern for the titles of Harry Potter books is: "Harry Potter and Something You Have Not Heard Of Before You Read This Book" If the pattern holds true, then we will be introduced to "The Half-Blood Prince" for the first time in book six. (Pip R. Lagenta, http://home.comcast.net/~galentripp/pip.htm l)

- J. K. Rowling may have made a Freudian slip when she wrote in September that she "actually voted in the 'Who's the Half-Blood Prince?'" poll at MuggleNet. The sharp-eyed folks at Godric's Hollow pointed out that the only poll at MuggleNet was one asking about the identity of the lion-like person mentioned in the excerpt. (09/06/04, http://www.godrics-hollow.net/modules.php?name=AvantGo&file=print&sid=1907).

The HBP is Harry Potter

Some debate sprang up over whether Harry Potter should be considered a half-blood. Troels Forchhammer nailed this one in a debate with Smaug69.

Riddle explicitly - in CoS - states that:

"Because there are strange likenesses between us, Harry Potter. Even you must have noticed. Both half-bloods, orphans, raised by Muggles." (CoS-17 'The Heir of Slytherin') - my emphasis.

Thus Riddle's definition (as does mine) /includes/ someone born by a Muggle and a wizard but is not logically confined to that.

Even if he had referred only to himself as a half-blood (without speaking of Harry's descent) you could not have concluded as you do. In that case it would have been specific logical fallacy. If A implies B it is not possible to infer that B implies A - only that not B implies not A. Thus the only available statements that would have been logically true based on Riddle's statement would be that "someone born to a Muggle and a wizard is half-blood" and that "someone who is not half-blood can not have been born to a Muggle and a wizard".

Allow me to summaries:

You call Riddle a half-blood.

I call Riddle a half-blood.

The book calls Riddle a half-blood.

So far there is no preference to be found. Riddle's statement supports both of our definitions equally (as long as you choose to ignore that it includes Harry).

You say that Harry is not a half-blood . (message <5fe774aa.0407010512.2482fe6f@posting.google.com>)

I say Harry is a half-blood.

Dumbledore says Harry is a half-blood.

Tom Riddle says Harry is a half-blood.

JK Rowling says Harry is a half-blood.

Do you see a pattern?

My interest is how the term is used by the wizards in Potterverse - not how others might choose to interpret it. It is abundantly clear that in their usage Harry is very much a half-blood, regardless of whether their usage is ethical (I'd agree any day that it is a bigoted term as it is used in Potterverse).

And now, for a little logic lesson! Troels explains:

Muggle parent + wizard parent => half-blood

The converse is not true. The converse is

'half-blood => Muggle parent + wizard parent'

(The fallacy of affirming the consequent)

The inverse is

'Not (Muggle parent + wizard parent) => Not (half-blood)'

(The fallacy of denying the antecedent)

Both are logical fallacies.

The valid statement that can be inferred is the modus tollens:

'Not (half-blood) => Not (Muggle parent + wizard parent)"

[To learn more, see
<http://www.mdcc.edu/wolfson/departments/math/Content/People/Faculty/Sanch
ez/CLAST/3.%20%20Logic/01%20Logic%20Summary%202003.htm>
<http://tinyurl.com/22t2c>

And<http://www.ship.edu/~cgboeree/fallacies.html>

The HBP is Voldemort

Some people have a hard time shaking the idea that the Half-Blood Prince is Voldemort. Here's what J. K. Rowling had to say.

> Has Voldemort or Tom Riddle ever cared for or loved anyone? Now, that's a cracking question to end with—very good. No, never. [Laughter.] If he had, he couldn't possibly be what he is. You will find out a lot more about that. It is a good question, because it leads us rather neatly to Half Blood Prince, although I repeat for the millionth time that Voldemort is not the half blood prince, which is what a lot of people thought. He is definitely, definitely not. (Edinburgh Book Festival, 8/15/04, http://www.jkrowling.com/textonly/news_view.cfm?id=80)

The HBP is Lupin

One favorite theory is that the kindly professor Lupin is the Half-Blood Prince. After all, he's a were-wolf, half man, half wolf, and his first name (Remus) is the same as one of the twin Princes who founded the city of Rome. Case closed, right? And there are some more interesting facts … not least being a possible leak from J. K. Rowling herself!

J. K. ROWLING IS POSTING ON IRC CHAT #MUGGLENET

One particularly interesting scenario was put forward by Nicholas Murado, aka "Professor Glitch ErrorWeaver," who thought he spotted J.K. Rowling lurking on the Internet Relay Chat (IRC) channel #MuggleNet and making suggestive comments about Lupin. Rowling has confirmed on her website that she likes MuggleNet and has visited its chat rooms at least once, in March 2004.

> A few weeks ago I did something I've never done before and took a stroll into a Harry Potter chat room: specifically, MuggleNet's chat room. Although I was concerned to find that many of the moderators feel their spiritual home is Slytherin, this is a great site. Nobody was remotely interested in my theories about what's going to happen in book seven, though. In the end, I gave up trying to impart any gems of wisdom and joined in the discussion about SpongeBob SquarePants (don't ask) (jkrowling.com, 3/15/04, http://www.jkrowling.com/textonly/news_view.cfm?id=63)..

Did she come back? I reproduce Professor ErrorWeaver's theory here, with permission, in nearly complete form. This is a great example of logical reasoning and the use of primary sources.

> Go to the source! Don't rely on third-hand rumors. Find the original documents and draw your own conclusions.

On July 23rd, at 9:06 P.M. (Eastern Time), we caught our first glimpse of what we (myself and a few others) have declared as J.K. Rowling incognito.

Signs we know (read: have a ~98% certainty factor) that this is really J.K. Rowling:

- Her sheer persistence for discussing theory.

- The fact that her IP and hostname checks out.

- The fact she "backpedals" (to stay undercover) whenever someone starts catching on to her (may not be evident in this batch of logs).

- Her ability to formulate coherent thoughts (this should not even be a factor, but given the imposters we've seen in the past, it is).

- The fact she -NEVER- says "I am J.K. Rowling;" most imposters are usually real willing to exclaim who they (aren't).

- The things she says.

Obvious enough, right? -A few other things we feel it is best to not mention right now. Any time her IRC name is mentioned (be it through the log or someone else saying it) it will be displayed as "[Name Edited]". This is the least I can do to protect her identity, if in fact we -are- right.

All commentary listed in brackets ("[ ]") are -MY OWN-, and were not part of the original log. They can be found at the end of certain lines

Lastly, I wish to note that this log has been massively trimmed for relevancy and ease of reading.   Enjoy! =)

-Professor Glitch ErrorWeaver

[And I, in turn, have also done a great deal of editing, to focus the extensive dialog that follows on issues specifically and clearly related to "Half-Blood Prince." -- wfz]

* [Name Edited] has joined #mugglenet

([Name Edited]) anyone want to chat about book seven theories?

* [Name Edited] has joined #mugglenet

([Name Edited]) Hey everyone

([Name Edited]) I was reading a BBC transcript of a JKR interview just before OOTP was released

([Name Edited]) and she says something VERY interesting in it

([Name Edited]) she says...

([Name Edited]) "There is one thing that if anyone guessed I would be really annoyed as it is kind of the heart of it all. And it kind of explains everything and no one's quite got there but a couple of people have skirted it. So you know, I would be pretty miffed after 13 or 14 years of writing the books if someone just came along and said I think this will happen in book seven. Because it is too late, I couldn't divert now, everything has been buildi [IRC cuts off lengthy copy/pastes; I doubt she knew that]

([Name Edited]) what do you make of that people?

([Name Edited]) one thing that was guess solves all the mysteries together

([Name Edited]) i recommend you read the interview in it's full at http://news.bbc.co.uk/1/hi/entertainment/arts/3004456.stm [BBC News, 6/19/03]

([Name Edited]) she says there she's already written the final chapter of book seven

...

([Name Edited]) what do you think is the one important thing that ties it all together that no one's guessed?

([Name Edited]) (and please don't say it was all a dream... JKR doesn't write cheese)

(iamtheHBP) harry is really having a love affair with professor sprout?

(lily_potter_01) harry has a twin he is the goal in the burrow's attic lol

([Name Edited]) btw, I reckon Chapter 9 of GoF is VERY special

([Name Edited]) we all ought to read it again

([Name Edited]) JKR said in another interview back in 2001, that she had Chapter 9 of GOF was sooooo difficult for her to write that she had to rewrite it 1213 times, and almost considered just leaving it out and going onto Chapter 10 with a page saying "chapter 9 was too tricky to write".....

([Name Edited]) it means there's something in Chapter 9 that she had to write VERY VERY carefully

(PityPat) what are you getting at [Name Edited]???

([Name Edited]) what i am saying is PityPat, that there may be a big clue in Chapter 9 of GoF

([Name Edited]) LUPIN IS HALF BLOOD [Emphasis mine /wfz]

...

([Name Edited]) Does anyone know the story of the Prince and the Pauper?

([Name Edited]) Who were the first Princes of Rome?

([Name Edited]) it is but the essence that fails...

([Name Edited]) why did Dumbledore have a look of triumph when Harry told him Voldemort used his blood to overcome the barrier he had of touching Harry? Do I smell a conspiracy??????

...

([Name Edited]) Lupin is Halfblood [She loves saying this in the chat.]

([Name Edited]) JK would never admit she was JK on here

([Name Edited]) and she's probably show a surprising amount of knowledge on whatever the random topic is being discussed

([Name Edited]) even if it IS SpongeBob SquarePants

...

* [Name Edited] has joined #mugglenet

** At least ten lines of random chat **

([Name Edited]) Good Day people

** At least twelve more lines of random chat **

([Name Edited]) gets ignored completely again... [hahaha.]

([Name Edited]) LUPIN IS THE HALF BLOOD PRINCE [Much more blatant; it came very early in the [Name Edited] saga, back when noone realized [Name Edited] could be/is JKR]

...([Name Edited]) if you read that chat, JKR gives full answers to all the questions she gets

([Name Edited]) apart from the ONE question where they ask her what Lupin is

([Name Edited]) all she replies to that is "Half Blood"

([Name Edited]) and goes straight onto the next question

([Name Edited]) JKR said clearly in her most recent chat Lupin IS HALF BLOOD

([Name Edited]) she didnt say anymore on that at all

([Name Edited]) that was before she released the title

([Name Edited]) someone asked her on world book day chat

http://www.the-leaky-cauldron.org/JKRWorldBookDay2004.html

([Name Edited]) did you get this site?

24

([Name Edited]) the full chat is on that site

([Name Edited]) and it has some interesting stuff

([Name Edited]) it happened in March of this year

([Name Edited]) so it's definitely worth reading through

([Name Edited]) here we have it

([Name Edited]) Siriusstar: Is Remus a pureblood?

([Name Edited]) JKR > Half Blood.

...([Name Edited]) JKR quotes: JKR (Lupin is) half blood.... JKR I absolutely love Professor Lupin

Amendment #1: On August 5th, [Professor Glitch ErrorWeaver] private messaged her. Here is the transcript of [their] chat.

...

[20:55:12] (ProfGlitch) suffice it to say, there are a few of us who have a nagging suspicion about you.

[20:55:40] (Name-Edited-Out) and what may that be? ...

[21:00:05] (ProfGlitch) lets just say there arent many imposters from london.02.net and who can formulate a proper grammatical sentence

[21:00:20] (ProfGlitch) to have had visited here.

[21:00:29] (Name-Edited-Out) oh dear

[Nothing more conclusive is said. – wfz.]

(http://www.livejournal.com/users/quidditchmaster/20806.html)

PERSPECTIVES ON THE LUPIN THEORY

Not everyone is enthusiastic about the Lupin theory. Some people who like Lupin found it rather ominous that he should be the center of attention. Usenet poster systahq observed:

[T]he only thing that would worry me about Lupin being the hbp is the fact that those sorts of characters don't usually make out too well in epic adventure tales (when they're a supporting character rather than the main hero, that is).

Then again, Lupin's character already has 'sacrificial lamb' written all over him...and sharing a name with a famous mythological murder victim doesn't really help your chances in a book like this...*sigh*

As long as Rowling keeps him around until the *very last page* of the*very last book* and *then* murders him horribly, then i won't gnash my teeth *too* much. well, not very loudly, anyway. probably only for a few weeks. (alt.fan.harry-potter, 8/10/04)

Other Usenet posters were concerned that the Lupin storyline would be too similar to a favorite storyline from J.R.R. Tolkien's Lord of the Rings. Miranda Schumacher expressed it nicely:

> We'll see. :)The refrain that Lupin is the half blood prince worries me slightly: A shabbily-dressed stranger whom the young heroes don't at first trust; who lives on the fringe of society, practically shunned, turns out to be of royal lineage. Even if this is a well-used motif in literature, it sort of screams Strider/Aragorn to me.

Catherine Johnson chimed in with a more sanguine viewpoint:

> And that's... a bad thing?

ITS NOT LUPIN'S TWIN, EITHER

"No," J. K. Rowling tells us on her web site, Professor Lupin does not have a twin. So the non-existent twin can't be the HBP.   : She also offers a tip: learn a little about Greek and Roman history! It's fun.

> No, but this obviously sprang from the fact that Lupin's Christian name (Remus) comes from one of the mythical founders of Rome who had a twin called 'Romulus'. (They were raised by wolves, incidentally).

The HBP is Hagrid

Hagrid is established as "half-blood" in the sense of half-human, half-giant, and is a favorite character. So it was natural that speculation would swirl around him.

Live Journal poster Nat had an amusing perspective on Hagrid.

> HAGRID? He's the, er, biggest half-blood of them all. He could be crowned Half-blood Prince of the Giants! No? Okay, maybe not, but it sounds neat to me. He still has Grawp around, after all, and he could take Grawp back to the giants and Grawp would be all, "Yo, this dog is da shizzle" and the giants would be like, "Wanna hang wit da posse?" and Hagrid would be all, "Yeah, I'm down wit dat" ... But we don't find out Hagrid is a half-blood until book 4. So. Maybe not.

One piece of negative evidence came up in September 2004, when MuggleNet reported:

> Two separate MuggleNet readers have written in to say that JK Rowling ruled out Hagrid as a possible Half-Blood Prince candidate at the Edinburgh book reading last August. She revealed this to both readers independently after being asked in the book tent. Thanks, Glenn and Bridget, for sharing this with us!

> Note that we cannot say with 100% accuracy this is true, but both readers had UK-based IP addresses and solid alibis. Consider this a good rumor, but not

yet a fact. (MuggleNet, 9/13/03,
http://www.mugglenet.com/newsfusion/fullnews.php?id=127)

The HBP is Sirius Black

Don't count on it. He's most likely dead. For confirmation, check out this comment by J. K. Rowling in discussing a Sirius Black web site, Immeritus (http://pages.prodigy.net/siriusblack/).

> I love this site, which I discovered towards the end of writing Order of the Phoenix, and which made me feel exceptionally guilty, as you can imagine. I am so proud of the fact that a character, whom I always liked very much, though he never appeared as much more than a brooding presence in the books, has gained a passionate fan-club.

The HBP is Sirius Black's son

Usenet poster Paul Wartenberg came up with this dandy theory:

> I think Sirius had an out-of-wedlock son with a Muggle woman, and with his death this son becomes the Heir to the Ancient and Noble House of Black.

> I'm not talking about Sirius' brother I'm talking about him possibly having a Muggle-born son! It would explain why Sirius rejected his family's obsession with purebloods and hatred of half-bloods and Muggles, by the fact of him falling in love with a young Muggle girl. That's what I'm focusing on. (Usenet, 6/30/04).

Don't bet on it. The problem is this theory is that it requires inventing too many new facts.

Sirius Black's dead brother, Regulus?

One theory revolves around Sirius Black's dead brother, Regulus. This suggestive name is reminiscent of the twin brothers Romulus and Remus who founded Rome. Regulus is famous in Roman history as a man of principle. He was captured in war by the Roman enemy, Carthage. I tell the story here because I think it's good for young readers to be exposed to the classics.

> Regulus remained in captivity for the next five years, till 250, when the Carthaginians, after their defeat by the proconsul Metellus, sent an embassy to Rome to solicit peace, or at least an exchange of prisoners. They allowed Regulus to accompany the ambassadors on the promise that he would return to Rome if their proposals were declined, thinking that he would persuade his countrymen to agree to an exchange of prisoners in order to obtain his own liberty.

> This mission of Regulus is one of the most celebrated stories in Roman history. The orators and poets related how Regulus at first refused to enter the city as a slave of the Carthaginians; how afterwards he would not give his opinion

in the Senate, as he had ceased by his captivity to be a member of that illustrious body; how, at length, when he was allowed by the Romans to speak, he endeavoured to dissuade the Senate from assenting to a peace, or even to an exchange of prisoners, and when he saw them wavering, from their desire of redeeming him from captivity, how he told them that the Carthaginians had given him a slow poison, which would soon terminate his life; and how, finally, when the Senate through his influence refused the offers of the Carthaginians, he firmly resisted all the persuasions of his friends to remain in Rome, and returned to Carthage, where a martyr's death awaited him.

On his arrival at Carthage he is said to have been put to death with the most excruciating tortures. (Hannibal Barca and the Punic Wars, http://www.barca.fsnet.co.uk/regulus.htm)

Unfortunately, the Regulus as HBP theory has some major shortcomings. Firstly, Regulus is supposed to be dead, and Sirius himself said that Regulus was not important in the story.

"Richard Eney" <dicconf@radix.net> wrote in message news:<10e4ict9oo8hqc4@corp.supernews.com>...

For Regulus to have been a half blood, Mrs Black would have to be wrong or lying about the Blacks all being pureblood and her side of the family also all being pureblood. Otherwise I'd love the idea of Regulus somehow being alive and the HBP, because of his name.

The HBP is Salazar Slytherin

Speculation quickly began to emerge that the half-blood prince was in some way related to Salazar Slytherin, one of the founders of Hogwarts and the inspiration of the House that bears his name. Usenet poster Kish suggested that:

"Prince" could stand for "Heir of Salazar Slytherin." (alt.fan.harry-potter, 6/28/04).

Then BaronjosefR took it a step further.

Anyone consider that Salazar Slytherin is the HBP? We know that the entire series is mostly generated by Slytherin's actions centuries before, yet we don't know much about him. Why? Maybe it is time we learned more about "Salazar Slytherin's noble work."

So, pertinent questions that remain unanswered:

What cause the schism that required Slytherin to leave Hogwarts? After years of accepting half-bloods into the school, why did he just up and leave when he has his own house that he could control?

What happened to him after he left? Did he just fall off the face of the earth?

Where did he come from? How identical are Voldy and Slytherin? Could they also match bloodlines?

> Salazar is the HBP. I am certain of it, (alt.fan.harry-potter, 6/28/04).

The most compelling argument against Salazar Slytherin as the HBP is that, well, he died, like, a thousand years ago. But some historically-minded Potter fans had an answer to that.

> I'm surmising that the "half-blood prince" is either Godric Gryffindor or Salazar Slytherin. Salazar could be disowning a hated Muggle ancestry in much the same way Tom Riddle did. JKR is using a working title from CoS for this book; and CoS was the book where the Founders were most prominently mentioned. I surmise that this means we will find out more about the Founders, what led to their split, and what Harry must do to heal the rift... I believe [The HBP] is a historical figure, and HBP is going to be focused more on the Founders.

> Woohoo! History! Says the history geek. (www.sugarquill.net, 6/30/04).

I love history, too, but I don't think this is going to be a time-machine story. ✗

The HBP is Godric Gryffindor

Another line of speculation is that the "half-blood prince" is somehow related to Godric Gryffindor.

As with the Salazar theory, the most compelling argument against Godric as HBP is that in all likelihood, Godric Gryffindor has been dead for a very long time. But Potter theorists quickly came up with a way of getting around that argument.

Sonja at MuggleNet speculated:

> ... Is it possible that Godric's mother had an affair with a Muggle that was kept a secret for along time, only to be discovered by Slytherin? It could be possible that's what caused the falling out.

> There is a lot of speculation that Harry is the true heir of Gryffindor. If that is true that would mean that James was also an heir, but not the "true heir." Is it possible that for there to be the "true heir of Gryffindor" that Harry had to be a half blood just like Godric? Only time, and of course Miss Rowling, will tell. (MuggleNet, 7/4/04, http://www.mugglenet.com/editorials/theburrow/sonja01.shtml)

Jason, a reader of the The Potter Profile, alertly noticed a good clue in the movie of Chamber of Secrets:

> [T]he huge , yet small, evidence I found was: In the movie, and book, the sword of Godric Gryffindor was pulled out of the Sorting Hat, and Dumbledore said it takes a true Gryffindor to pull that sword out of the hat. Well, if indeed Harry is the heir, that means if Harry is half blood, then ... Godric Gryffindor ... is possible. Somehow, there is a connection between Godric and the HBP, ... (The Potter Profile, http://www.thepotterprofile.com/hbptheories.php?=0)

Potter fan Carrie in her blog "I Solemnly Swear I am Up to No Good" (great name!) came up with a good "trust Rowling" argument against the Godric as HBP theory.

> If Rowling had not said she removed all traces of the Half Blood Prince storyline from CoS, I would be 100% behind Godric Gryffindor as the Half Blood Prince, but that little fact makes me doubt it. And while just being in CoS wouldn't necessarily preclude someone from being the HPB, Godric Gryffindor was introduced in CoS in a way that completely tied him into the basilisk/Tom Riddle storyline, which Rowling also said the HPB had nothing to do with. (http://www.so-now-im-a-freak.com/harry/, 8/06/04).

The "Godric Gryffindor" angle picked up some energy when the "tawny-haired man" excerpt was released. Lions, courage, Gryffindor … ?

The HBP is Dudley Dursley

Some attention focused on perhaps the least likable character in the series, Dudley Dursley. For example, Usenet poster Mondayitis put together the following set of clues. He begins with an admirable disclaimer.

> First off, this is not my own original idea. I read a post that > mentioned it and it just clicked with me - it all fits so nicely. Here are my puzzle pieces ...- Dudley is a pampered prince.- Aunt Petunia's strange reactions at the beginning of OotP which hinted at her possibly knowing more about wizarding life than she lets on. –
>
> JKR's 2 hints
>
> we will soon learn more about Lily's past (and therefore obviously her sister Petunia's past.)
>
> 2. in the B&N chat in 1999 JKR says ... "In my books, magic almost always shows itself in a person before age 11; however, there is a character who does manage in desperate circumstances to do magic quite late in life, but that is very rare in the world I am writing about."
>
> Putting all that together my guess is that Petunia will accidentally perform magic (perhaps in an attempt to save Harry) over the summer. This would be a great lead in to learning about Lily's past – perhaps seven telling us about the famous green eye references. It would also show Petunia to be a squib not a Muggle proving little Dudders to be a half blood … Anyone with me?

In other words, lemmings, follow me to the cliff! Poster Delta5MQ pointed out one obvious flaw:

> I would be [with you] save the fact Duds can't see dementors.

But no! Poster GJW to the rescue of Dudley fans with this insightful comment.

We don't know that for sure. Remember that it was pitch dark when the Dementors attacked him (and Harry), and at first both he and Harry were blinded. Harry couldn't see them either, he only recognized them from their effect (the cold, the sound of their breathing) because he had experienced them before. Harry eventually lit his wand and was then able to see them, but by then Dudley was curled up in a ball, his arms clamped over his face, and wasn't trying to see anything...

So it's quite possible that Dudley _can_ see Dementors.

In fact, I'd say it may be likely. Why? JKR seems to have gone out of her way to make sure Dudley couldn't see anything. In the past books, the Dementors were not accompanied by total, blinding darkness at the very onset. Why were they this time? And why is it conveniently mentioned that Dudley has his arms clamped across his face? JKR may well have been giving Dudley an excuse for not seeing the Dementors, so that we wouldn't realize that he could...

Of course, for Dudley to be a half-blood, Lily would have to be a witch. And that hasn't been established yet. And may not be.

(Yes, I'm ruling out the possibility that Vernon is a wizard. I think that would be stretching things just a little too much. ;) (Usenet, 7/4/04)

Much fun was had imagining Dudley as a newly revealed half-blood prince.

- Dudley to Hogwarts with Harry as his bodyguard.

- Dudley as a spare for Neville Longbottom's toad, Trevor.

- Dudley as a protégé of the Weasley brothers, Fred and George.

At the Edinburgh Book Fair in August 2004, J. K. Rowling put a big spike in the Dudley as HBP theory.

Is Aunt Petunia a Squib?

Good question. No, she is not, but—[Laughter]. No, she is not a Squib. She is a Muggle, but—[Laughter]. You will have to read the other books. You might have got the impression that there is a little bit more to Aunt Petunia than meets the eye, and you will find out what it is. She is not a squib, although that is a very good guess. Oh, I am giving a lot away here. I am being shockingly indiscreet. (Edinburgh Book Festival, 8/15/2004, http://www.jkrowling.com/textonly/news_view.cfm?id=80).

And then, even more definitively:

Is there more to Dudley than meets the eye?

No. [Laughter]. What you see is what you get. I am happy to say that he is definitely a character without much back story. He is just Dudley. The next book, Half Blood Prince, is the least that you see of the Dursleys. You see them quite briefly. You see them a bit more in the final book, but you don't get a lot of Dudley in book six—very few lines. I am sorry if there are Dudley fans out there, but I think you need to look at your priorities if it is Dudley that you are looking forward to. [Laughter].(Edinburgh Book Festival, 8/15/2004, http://www.jkrowling.com/textonly/news_view.cfm?id=80).

But Rowling's perspective on Dudley really goes deeper.

I feel sorry for Dudley. I might joke about him, but I feel truly sorry for him because I see him as just as abused as Harry. Though, in possibly a less obvious way. What they are doing to him is inept, really. I think children recognize that. Poor Dudley. He's not being prepared for the world at all, in any reasonable or compassionate way, so I feel sorry for him. (Cinescape, 11/16/00, http://www.cinescape.com/0/editorial.asp?aff_id=0&jump=next&obj_id=26474&this_cat=Books).

Although she felt impelled to add:

But there's something funny about him, also. The pig's tail was irresistible.`

The HBP is <insert Highly Obscure Character Here>

Theories were advanced in favor of every obscure character in the series.

THE HBP IS DEAN THOMAS

Good grief. Could there be any more obscure theory? Well, yes…

Well, on her website, JKR does talk about Dean Thomas' background which was dropped from CoS and how she focused more on Neville from that point. Dean was supposed to be much more prominent so I'm guessing that he might be the half-blood prince. Of course, JKR could be going a completely different route with the idea. smaug69

THE HBP IS MARK EVANS.

Over-alert readers noticed that the boy who is beaten up by Dudley in chapter one of Order of the Phoenix (OOTP) is named Mark Evans, and that Lily Potter's name before marriage was Evans. Instant theory! Mark Evans is the HBP. Unfortunately for these folks, J. K. Rowling promptly shot the theory down in highly definitive manner.

Mark Evans is… nobody. He's nobody in the sense that Mr. Prentice, Madam Marsh and Gordon-Dudley's-gang-member are nobodies, just background people who need names, but who have no role other than the walk-on parts assigned to them. …

I've got nobody to blame but myself. Sirius Black, Mrs. Figg and Mundungus Fletcher were all mentioned in passing well before they burst onto the stage as fully-fledged characters, so now you've all become too clever, not for your own good, but for mine. The fact is that once you drew my attention to it, I realised that Mark Evans did indeed look like one of those 'here he is, just a casual passer-by, nothing to worry about, bet you barely noticed him' characters who would suddenly become, half way through book seven, 'Ha ha! Yes, Mark Evans is back, suckers, and he's the key to everything! He's the Half Blood Prince, he's Harry's Great-Aunt, he's the Heir of Gryffindor, he lives up the Pillar of Storgé and he owns the Mystic Kettle of Nackledirk!' (Possible title of book seven there, must make a note of it).

Then why – WHY – (I hear you cry) – did I give him the surname "Evans"? Well, believe me, you can't regret it more than I do right now. "Evans" is a common name; I didn't give it much thought; I wasn't even trying to set up another red herring. I could just as easily have called him 'Smith' or 'Jones' (or 'Black' or 'Thomas' or 'Brown', all of which would have got me into trouble too). (jkrowling.com, http://www.jkrowling.com/textonly/faq_view.cfm?id=49)

THE HBP IS SEAMUS FINNEGAN

My money is on it being Seamus. Remember just after the sorting in the first book? Seamus states that his mother is a witch and his dad is a Muggle, also that it was a bit of a shock for his dad because she didn't tell him till after they were married :D LOL. [Die Laughing Out Loud—wfz]

Can you imagine Seamus as a Prince? Weird. (Usenet poster Stargirl alt.fan.harry-potter, 74/04).

VIKTOR KRUM

Perhaps Viktor will come back?

But Viktor is at Durmstrang, and we know that Durmstrang only accepts purebloods. John Fisher   john@drummond.demon.co.uk

The HBP is someone silly

Downright silly theories were also advanced by those in a whimsical mood.

THE HBP IS HERMAN GRANGER.

[Hermione Granger] is really a boy in disguise. Her real name is HERMAN Granger! Imagine Ron and Harry's surprise! (Grant Davis, 10, Plano (Dallas Morning News, July 23, 2004)

THE HBP IS GREAT BRITAIN'S MUGGLE PRINCE CHARLES

Complete with jughead ears. ✗

So who is NOT the half-blood prince?

With all the speculation about possible candidates, some evidence did emerge that allowed particular possibilities to be ruled out.

He is NOT Harry and he is NOT Voldemort

J. K. Rowling swiftly shot down two of the most obvious possibilities.

> As a little bonus, and compensation for having been messed around by Mr. or Ms. Storgé, I shall tell you one thing without making you shift any bricks at all: the HBP is neither Harry nor Voldemort. And that's all I'm saying on THAT subject until the book's published.
> http://www.jkrowling.com/textonly/news_view.cfm?id=77

Even in the face of this seemingly clear answer, readers fought the facts.

> Something that occurred to me while I was cleaning and finding a new home for my Harry Potter books. JKR has already said that Harry Potter and the Half-Blood Prince is the title of the sixth book, and that was the original title for Chamber of Secrets. She's also said that the title has nothing to do with Harry or Voldemort. BUT, she didn't say it didn't have anything to do with Tom Riddle. Yes, Tom and Voldy are technically the same person, but knowing JKR's mind games, it would be such a simple answer. Because really, WHO ELSE is important in Chamber? No one. I've read that book more than all of the others, as it is my favorite. Unless she's referring to Lockhart, which would bring me SO MUCH JOY, the half-blood prince is [95% sure] Tom Riddle. Or perhaps Lucius... but oh, that is blasphemy, as Lucius Malfoy is the KING OF PUREBLOODS.
>
> If this was obvious to anyone else, sorry. My brain processes things very slow. I didn't even see the death in Order of the Phoenix coming, even though everyone else I talked to said it was the most obvious of things.
> (http://www.livejournal.com/users/sake_butterfly/362883.html)

He is NOT a dwarf

Amazingly, eight people in the poll at wfzimmerman.com (see below) believed that the "Half-Blood Prince" might be a dwarf. There *are* dwarves in J. K. Rowling's world—they make a brief cameo appearance early in "Chamber of Secrets"—but they could hardly be more obscure.

He is NOT Neville's toad Trevor

In the early excitement over the HBP title, Usenet poster Jena offered up this unlikely theory:

> How about Trevor? That's Neville's frogs name right? It's about time that poor little amphibian got some good storyline ;)(alt.fan.harry-potter, 6/28/04).

"Sebapop" elaborated:

> Ha! Neville's toad, Trevor, is an animagus. Hermione is going to kiss Neville but the toad will jump right there, so Hermione will kiss the toad. The toad-wizard will remember the fact that he was once a human being and he will get back into his shape: a really ugly half blood wizard prince. He will fall in love with Hermione, but she will refuse him. Madly in love and furious with her, he will disappear into the> Forbidden Forest. He will get in touch with the Death Eaters - Voldy wanted a mushroom soup and that kind of mushrooms grows only in the Forbidden Forest, what a coincidence, uh? - and be convinced that he> will get Hermione if he helps them killing Harry Potter.

> Tah dah! Harry Potter and the half-blood prince.

> Sebastiano (alt.fan.harry-potter, 6/29/04)

He is NOT a composite of Prince William and the Artist Formerly Known As ...

One LiveJournal user came up with a composite image of Britain's handsome Prince William, Minnesota's eccentric singer Prince, and Harry Potter's lightning-bolt scar. (http://www.livejournal.com/users/wikdsushi/464171.html)

The HBP is NOT Professor Flitwick ...

> Not unless HBP stands for **H**itler-esque **B**lack-haired **P**int-sizer! (Maybe it was one of those things in the third movie that foreshadowed Book 6?)<groan> (Usenet poster Chistaya, alt.fan.harry-potter, 7/7/04). ✗

Totally unscientific poll results

The results of a totally unscientific poll taken at wfzimmerman.com.

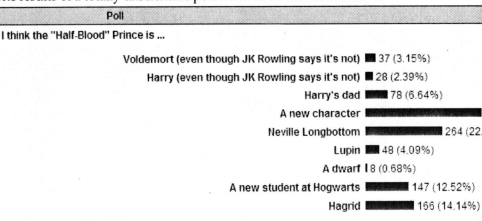

Figure 3. These results are less than unscientific. ✔

What will the sixth book NOT be called?

- "Harry Potter and the Green Flame Torch"

- "Harry Potter and the Mountain of Fantasy"

- "Harry Potter and the Fortress of Shadows"

- "Harry Potter and the Forest of Shadows"

All these titles have been definitively nixed by J.K. Rowling on her website. Interestingly, she wrote:

> And this green torch business seems to be cropping up everywhere. Do you really think getting rid of Voldemort would be that easy? (jkrowling.com, http://www.jkrowling.com/textonly/rumours_view.cfm?id=10)

- "The Pillar of Storgé"

J.K. Rowling wrote on her website:

> I am trying very hard not to feel offended that anyone thought this was possible. 'Storgé', for crying out loud. Come on, people, get a grip. (jkrowling.com, http://www.jkrowling.com/textonly/rumours_view.cfm?id=21)

A skeptical view from unrepentant adult Allan Brown: "Rumour had suggested the book would rejoice in the title Harry Potter and the Pillar of Storgé. The author, though, described this as 'laughable', as though the word Storgé were more risible than the words Weasley, Quidditch or Gryffindor."

- "The Toenail of Icklibõgg"

> Well, if you believed the 'Storgé' one... (jkrowling.com, http://www.jkrowling.com/textonly/rumours_view.cfm?id=22)

- "Harry Potter and the Philosopher's Stoning"

> "Quite against my hope that she'd address the current situation in Iran by titling it Harry Potter and the Philosopher's Stoning...", JK has gone instead for "Harry Potter and the Half Blood Prince." (Sunday Times, 07/04/2004)

- "Harry Potter and the Temple of Doom."

> I'm old-fashioned enough to want book 6 to be *Harry Potter and the Temple of Doom* and book 7 to be *Harry Potter and the Last Crusade*, but I expect to be disappointed here.]http://www.livejournal.com/users/rysmiel/225147.html

- "Harry Potter and the Harry Potter"

When wise-cracking former ESPN anchor Keith Olbermann heard that J. K Rowling "wouldn't give any other details, save to say that the half blood prince of "**Harry Potter**" and the half blood prince is neither Lord Voldemort, nor Harry himself," he commented:

> Well, of course it isn't Harry himself, woman. That would make the title of the book "Harry Potter and the Harry Potter." What do I have to do, write these blessed books for you? ("Countdown," MSNBC, June 30, 2004). ✗

How long will the book be?

Stephen Fry, the audio book narrator, says:

> "I think we can probably say that this next one is probably not going to be longer than the 'Order of the Phoenix' - 29 hours of listening if you buy the tapes or CDs. That's a lot of studio time reading!" (BBC Radio, 07/01/04, http://www.bbc.co.uk/radio1/news/entertainment/040701_harrypotter.shtml)

J. K. Rowling is trying to keep HBP shorter than OOTP.

> Is every book going to be bigger than the previous one?
>
> No, definitely not, or book seven would be around the weight of a baby hippopotamus. According to the plan for book six, it will be quite a bit shorter than 'Order of the Phoenix'. I am not going to swear on my children's lives that that is going to be the case, but I am 99% certain of it. (jkrowling.com, http://www.jkrowling.com/textonly/faq_view.cfm?id=35).

As far as page count goes, remember that number of pages in a book can vary dramatically depending on the trim size of the book (how big it is), font size (how big the letters are), and the margins (narrow, medium, or wide). As a reference point,, the U.S. Scholastic hard-cover version of Order of the Phoenix was 870 printed pages, and the U.K. Bloomsbury hard-cover was 766 pages

What will the cover look like?

Take a look at 20 beautiful hypothetical covers done by Mugglenet fans at http://www.mugglenet.com/hbpcontest/. ✎

How popular will HBP be?

In the eight weeks since British author Joanne "J.K." Rowling set up her personal website, it has received an astonishing 220 million visits.

Fans have clicked onto the website from 236 countries, including Iraq, Christmas Island and the Vatican. (Daily Telegraph, 7/04)

By most counts, that's more countries than there are in the world! The United Nations only thinks it has 191 members (http://www.un.org/Overview/unmember.html).

HBP's GoogleCount tracks the news

The GoogleCount for "Half-Blood Prince" measures the number of web pages using that exact term. As the chart below shows, the number of pages goes up and down in response to news developments (there was a big peak in mid-August shortly after J. K. Rowling spoke at the Edinburgh Book Festival).

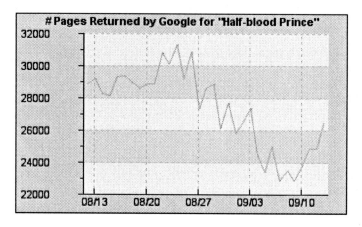

Figure 4. GoogleCount for "Half-Blood Prince" by g-metrics.com.

How many copies will Half-Blood Prince sell?

The numbers are staggerositous (a made-up word combining "staggering" and "preposterous."

Incredibly, in just seven years since the launch of her first story, the Perthshire-based writer has just seen sales of her Harry Potter books top 260 million copies worldwide - more than the total viewers in the world who have ever seen The Muppets.

JK's agent, Christopher Little, announced the huge sales following the release last Saturday of the paperback version of Harry Potter and the Order of the Phoenix.

"The sales show no sign of slowing down - in fact the opposite as more young children enter the reading age and parents catch-up, " said a spokesman for publishers Bloomsbury.

"The books have now sold more than 260 million copies and there are still two more to come in the series."...

However, the Bible remains the best selling book of all time. Nobody has an exact idea about how many have been sold, but estimates vary between 2.5 billion and 6 billion copies in its various translations. Some 170,000 Bibles are distributed each day in the US alone.

To give a scale of JK's achievement there is now more than one copy of Harry Potter to every four televisions in the world.

A spokeswoman for JK declined to comment on the author's sales but said she was "hard at work" on the next book, **Harry Potter and The Half Blood Prince,** and was "enjoying writing it." (Express, July 19, 2004)

First day numbers are ginormous.

The latest instalment -- The Order of the Phoenix -- sold 1.78 million copies on its first day in Britain. (Waikato Times, N.Z., July 3, 2004)

Even pre-orders set records.

Amazon. co.uk took more than 420,000 pre-orders for the most recent book in JK Rowling's series, Harry Potter & The Order Of The Phoenix. (Express, July 6, 2004)

It's impossible to know for sure, but my guess is that the last two books in the series will sell as many as the first five books combined. ✔

HBP: The Movie

Release date according to the Internet Movie Database Professional version (IMDBpro.com): November 2008.

The early buzz

In September 2004, the HBP movie was already beginning to generate some buzz on the Internet Movie Database's MovieMeter (http://pro.imdb.com/title/tt0417741/).

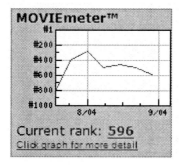

Figure 5. IMDB searches on "Harry Potter and the Half-Blood Prince."

In Sep. 2004, "Harry Potter and the Half-Blood Prince" was rated 596—not bad for a movie due four years in the future! By way of comparison, brand names like "X-Men 3" and "Spiderman 3" ranked at 177 and 317, even though they were expected to release a year or two earlier.

An amusing detail is that JK Rowling's pregnancy caused a noticeable upward spike in audience awareness of her future movie.

Date	Rank	Events
2004 Aug 29	596	
2004 Aug 22	634	
2004 Aug 15	525	
2004 Aug 8	312	
2004 Aug 1	281	⌂ JK Rowling Pregnant
2004 Jul 25	387	
2004 Jul 18	804	

Figure 6. IMDB rank for the HBP movie.

The cast

The movie won't enter production for a couple of years, but some intelligent speculation about the cast is possible.

THE THREE FRIENDS

Harry, Hermione, and Ron are the core of the series, and of the movies. But it's well known that teen actors go through many changes, and to wonder whether they will all remain in their roles until the completion of movie #7. For what it's worth, J. K. Rowling has made her feelings known.

> Coolbeans3131: Would you like to see the same actors portray the trio in all 7 movies?

> JK Rowling replies -> Yes, I would. I really like all three of them. (World Book Day chat, 3/04/04, http://www.wizardnews.com/story.200403042.html),

Let's hope it works out that way. They're all terrific young actors.

VOLDEMORT

In all likelihood, the English actor Ralph Fiennes will play Lord Voldemort in the movie of "Half-Blood Prince." Fiennes has signed a contract to play He Who Must Not Be Named (Except By Really Super-Courageous Characters) in the movie of "Goblet of Fire." Unless Fiennes is terrible, gets sick, or succumbs to rampaging ego (that would never happen to Voldemort), he will probably be Voldemort all the way through the end of the series.

So who is Ralph Fiennes? The most notable credits in his 25+ film appearances since 1990 are "Schindler's List," (1993) where he played an evil German concentration camp officer; "The English Patient" (1996), where he was the leading man; and "Red Dragon" (2002), where he played a murderer so heinous that Hannibal Lecter had to kill him. More to the point, what is he like, and what will he be like as Voldemort?

Most basically, he is a very good-looking movie star. More specifically, he has intriguing features that combine refinement and brutality. He looks sensitive as hell, but he also looks like he can be a real son-of-a-bitch.

He can look very English – even aristocratic. This is interesting since we learn in "Chamber of Secrets" and "Goblet of Fire" that in fact, Tom Riddle is not an aristocrat. He is a half-blood ... but not, as far as we know, a prince.

Can you imagine this? Fiennes was nervous about signing up to play the most villainous villain in the history of bad guys, He Who Must Not Be Named. (http://www.femalefirst.co.uk/entertainment/2832004.htm)

Michael Moore will not be directing the movie of "Harry Potter and the Half-Blood Prince"

A bizarre rumor went around in July 2004 that the American documentary writer Michael Moore ("Fahrenheit 9/11") would be directing the movie of HBP. Moore is famous for angry political rants against Republicans and giant corporations using handheld camera and "ambush" interviews.

> Various film websites are reporting that documentary writer/producer/director Michael Moore has been invited to direct the film version of book VI.
>
> It appears to us that this rumor got started when satirical news site the Spoof "reported" the "news". Chinese news site Xinhuanet.com apparently then picked up the story and reported it as fact. It has since spread to film and news sites too numerous to mention.
>
> We could post a lengthy discussion as to the many reasons this report must surely be a baseless rumor... http://www.the-leaky-cauldron.org/MTarchives/week_2004_07_04.html#004866

LiveJournal poster BethBethBeth came up with a brilliant vision of the Michael Moore treatment of "Half-Blood Prince."

> Moore: "...and so we went to the first place you'd want to go if you were looking for a Half-Blood Prince: my home town, Flint, Michigan."
> http://www.livejournal.com/users/bethbethbeth/116241.html?#cutid1

Fans, rest easy. The director won't be Michael Moore.

It's too early to tell who will be directing movie #6.. Indian director Mira Nair has been asked to direct "Harry Potter and the Order of the Phoenix." A puzzling choice, since this Indian-born director doesn't seem like a particularly good fit. Her previous credits include "Salaam Bombay" (about children on the streets of Bombay), "Mississippi Masala" (Indian family moves from Uganda to Mississippi), and "Vanity Fair" (social climber in 1800s England). The only one that really seems to have any relevance is "Vanity Fair," and that has gotten mixed reviews ... many reviewers think she missed the point of the book. Let's hope she gets the point of Harry Potter. To be fair, there's reason to hope that she will. She admitted in an early interview:

> "My son Zoharan's excited. I've seen all the Harry Potter movies with him." (Guardian, http://film.guardian.co.uk/news/story/0,12589,1295660,00.html)

That's a good sign. Fingers crossed, everyone! ⋈

Part Two—Harry Potter books six and seven

Why talk about books six and seven together

At this point, with both books six and seven still yet to come, there are a great many important questions that will be answered either in book six or book seven—but no one except J. K. Rowling knows which! So this part of the book talks about all the major unresolved issues of the series *except* those which J. K. Rowling has specifically said will only be resolved in book seven. ✗

Things we will definitely see in either book six or book seven

There are a lot of important things that we know for sure we will find out in either"Harry Potter and the Half-Blood Prince" or Harry Potter book seven.

The answer to the "two questions"

One of the very most important clues that J. K. Rowling has ever offered to the mystery underlying the end of the series came near the end of her chat at the Edinburgh Book Festival in August 2004.

> I thought that I would give you something though, rather than get to the end of today and think that I have not given you a lot. There are two questions that I have never been asked but that I should have been asked, if you know what I mean. If you want to speculate on anything, you should speculate on these two things, which will point you in the right direction.
>
> The first question that I have never been asked—it has probably been asked in a chatroom but no one has ever asked me—is, "Why didn't Voldemort die?" Not, "Why did Harry live?" but, "Why didn't Voldemort die?" The killing curse rebounded, so he should have died. Why didn't he?
>
> At the end of Goblet of Fire he says that one or more of the steps that he took enabled him to survive. You should be wondering what he did to make sure that he did not die—I will put it that way. I don't think that it is guessable. It may be—someone could guess it—but you should be asking yourself that question, particularly now that you know about the prophesy. I'd better stop there or I will really incriminate myself.
>
> The other question that I am surprised no one has asked me since Phoenix came out—I thought that people would—is why Dumbledore did not kill or try to kill Voldemort in the scene in the ministry. I know that I am giving a lot away to people who have not read the book. Although Dumbledore gives a kind of reason to Voldemort, it is not the real reason.
>
> When I mentioned that question to my husband—I told Neil that I was going to mention it to you—he said that it was because Voldemort knows that there are two more books to come. As you can see, we are on the same literary wavelength. [Laughter]. That is not the answer; Dumbledore knows something slightly more profound than that. If you want to wonder about anything, I would advise you to concentrate on those two questions. That might take you a little bit further. (Edinburgh Book Festival, 8/15/2004, http://www.jkrowling.com/textonly/news_view.cfm?id=80) ✗

More about Harry

Rowling has dropped various tidbits about things pertaining to Harry Potter's person. For example, his scar:

> Cathedral: Don't want to rune the ending, but will we be finding out more about the significance of the shape of Harry's scar in future books?
>
> JK Rowling: The shape is not the most significant aspect of that scar, and that's all I'm going to say! ! (World Book Day chat, 3/4/04, http://www.wizardnews.com/story.200403042.html)

And the color of his eyes:

> Sussie: Does Harry's eye colour become important in the future books, like we've heard?
>
> JK Rowling replies -> No comment! ! (World Book Day chat, 3/4/04, http://www.wizardnews.com/story.200403042.html)

Early in every book, there is a description of Harry's green eyes.

More about Snape, and less about bad boys ...

J. K. Rowling has promised that we will learn more about everyone's favorite nasty teacher.

> Also, will we see more of Snape?
>
> You always see a lot of Snape, because he is a gift of a character. I hesitate to say that I love him. [Audience member: I do]. You do? This is a very worrying thing. Are you thinking about Alan Rickman or about Snape? [Laughter]. Isn't this life, though? I make this hero—Harry, obviously—and there he is on the screen, the perfect Harry, because Dan is very much as I imagine Harry, but who does every girl under the age of 15 fall in love with? Tom Felton as Draco Malfoy. Girls, stop going for the bad guy. Go for a nice man in the first place. It took me 35 years to learn that, but I am giving you that nugget free, right now, at the beginning of your love lives.

And at the Edinburgh Book Festival she said:

> Apart from Harry, Snape is my favourite character because he is so complex and I just love him. Can he see the Thestrals, and if so, why? Also, is he a pure blood wizard?
>
> Snape's ancestry is hinted at. He was a Death Eater, so clearly he is no Muggle born, because Muggle-borns are not allowed to be Death Eaters, except in rare circumstances. You have some information about his ancestry there. He can see Thestrals, but in my imagination most of the older people at Hogwarts would be able to see them because, obviously, as you go through life you do lose people and understand what death is. But you must not forget that Snape was a Death Eater. He will have seen things that... Why do you love him? Why do

people love Snape? I do not understand this. Again, it's bad boy syndrome, isn't it? It's very depressing. [Laughter]. One of my best friends watched the film and she said, "You know who's really attractive?" I said, "Who?" She said, "Lucius Malfoy!" (Edinburgh Book Festival, 8/15/04).

Other things we'll see

A new Minister of Magic.

> Miggs: Is there going to be a new minister of magic in the next books?
>
> JK Rowling: Yes. Ha! Finally, a concrete bit of information, I hear you cry! (World Book Day chat, 3/4/04, http://www.wizardnews.com/story.200403042.html)

The fate of Sirius Black's flying motorbike.

> Rita: Whatever happened to Sirius' flying motorbike?
>
> JK Rowling:, good question. You'll find out, but the real sleuths among you might be able to guess! (World Book Day chat, 3/4/04, http://www.wizardnews.com/story.200403042.html)

The fate of Sirius's two-way mirror.

> Kelpie_8: Will the two way mirror Sirius gave Harry ever show up again?
>
> JK Rowling: Ooooo good question. There's your answer.! (World Book Day chat, 3/4/04, http://www.wizardnews.com/story.200403042.html)
>
> Why did Harry have to forget the mirror he had been given by Sirius in 'Order of the Phoenix'?
>
> I can't give a full answer to this, because it is relevant to books six and seven. However, the short answer is that Harry was determined never to use the mirror, as is clearly stated in chapter 24: 'he knew he would never use whatever it was'. For once in Harry's life, he does not succumb to curiosity, he hides the mirror and the temptation away from himself, and then, when it might have been useful, he has forgotten it.
>
> The mirror might not have helped as much as you think, but on the other hand, will help more than you think. You'll have to read the final books to understand that! (jkrowling.com, http://www.jkrowling.com/textonly/faq_view.cfm?id=22)

More about Tonks.

> LizardLaugh: I love Tonks, she's my favorite new character. Will she play a large role in future books and/or in Harry's life?JK Rowling replies -> Tonks is hanging around. I really like her, too. ! (World Book Day chat, 3/4/04, http://www.wizardnews.com/story.200403042.html)

Nothing whatsoever about Hermione and Draco Malfoy!

Chibimono: Do you have any future plans in particular for Draco Malfoy?

JK Rowling replies -> I've got plans for all my characters. Actually, this is a really good place to answer a question about Draco and Hermione, which a certain Ms. Radcliffe is desperate to have answered. Will they end up together in book six/seven? NO! The trouble is, of course, that girls fancy Tom Felton, but Draco is NOT Tom Felton! (My daughter likes TF very much too, because he taught her how to use a diablo)

Mad Eye Moody, just as we love and remember him.

SnapesForte: Is Mad Eye Moody the real Moody this time? And if he is, is he up to something fishy? Because he's acting too much like Crouch jr - sniffing food etc.

JK Rowling replies -> It's the other way around - Crouch Jnr. acted just like the real Moody. (World Book Day chat, 3/04/04, http://www.mugglenet.com/jkrwbd.shtml).

Much less about Cho Chang.

eastbrook4: why did Harry have to split up with Cho Chang?

JK Rowling replies -> That's life, I'm afraid. They were never going to be happy, it was better that it ended early! (World Book Day chat, 3/04/04, http://www.mugglenet.com/jkrwbd.shtml).

A little about Krum.

bertieana: Will we be seeing Krum again any time soon?

JK Rowling replies -> You will see Krum again, though not soon. (World Book Day chat, 3/04/04, http://www.mugglenet.com/jkrwbd.shtml).

More of Moaning Myrtle.

novell: I find moaning myrtle is the saddest character in your books, inspiring a mixture of revulsion and pity. Does she play any further part?

JK Rowling replies -> You do see her again. Don't you like her? I know she's a bit revolting, but that's why I'm so fond of her. (World Book Day chat, 3/04/04, http://www.mugglenet.com/jkrwbd.shtml).

Don't you wish you had been a fly on this wall?

Mugglenet Chatroom Uninterested in JKR's Theories

A few weeks ago I did something I've never done before and took a stroll into a Harry Potter chat room: specifically, MuggleNet's chat room. Although I was concerned to find that many of the moderators feel their spiritual home is Slytherin, this is a great site.

Nobody was remotely interested in my theories about what's going to happen in book seven, though.

Things we will NOT see in books six or seven

This is a good place to refute some of the more absurd rumors that you may have encountered. As Mark Twain said, it's not the things you don't know, it's the things you think you know that ain't so. Here are a few possibilities that will *not* happen.

Harry Potter's mother Lily as a nasty former Death Eater. In the "Rumours" section of her website, J. K. Rowling refutes the idea his way:

> How dare you?! (jkrowling.com, http://www.jkrowling.com/textonly/rumours_view.cfm?id=5).

Neville Longbottom as Peter Pettigrew's son. [Eww... gross! /wfz]

> See response for 'Lily Potter was a Death Eater' above. (jkrowling.com, http://www.jkrowling.com/textonly/rumours_view.cfm?id=8).

We will *not* see Harry become an animagus..

> Sean Bullard (NPR): We're going to take a few more questions and um, the next one is: "Will Harry ever turn into a *shape-changer* like his father?"

> J.K. Rowling: No, Harry's not in training to be an animagus. If you ... unless you've read book 3, you won't know ... that's a wizard that ... it's very, very difficult to do. They, they ... learn to turn themselves into animals. No, Harry is not ... Harry's energies are going to be concentrated elsewhere and he's not going to have time to do that. He's got quite a full agenda coming up, poor, poor boy. (National Press Club Luncheon, 10/20/99, http://www.hogwarts-library.net/reference/interviews/19991020_NPCLuncheon.html)

Harry as a relative of Voldemort.

> Is Voldemort some sort of relative of Harry's? Possibly his mother's brother?

> Rowling: I'm laughing...that would be a bit Star Wars, wouldn't it? (Scholastic live interview, 10/16/00, http://www.scholastic.com/harrypotter/author/transcript2.htm)

And, rebutting the rumor that "Voldemort is Harry's real father/grandfather/close relative of some description," J. K. Rowling got pretty excited:

> No, no, no, no, no. You lot have been watching much too much Star Wars. James is DEFINITELY Harry's father. Doesn't everybody Harry meets say 'you look just like your father'? And hasn't Dumbledore already told Harry that Voldemort is the last surviving descendent of Salazar Slytherin? Just to clarify - this means that Harry is NOT a descendent of Salazar Slytherin. (http://www.jkrowling.com/textonly/rumours_view.cfm?id=3)

Dumbledore as Harry's grandfather.

If Dumbledore had been Harry's grandfather, why on earth would he have been sent to live with the Dursleys? (jkrowling.com)

The long-lost love of Tom Riddle's life.

Has Voldemort or Tom Riddle ever cared for or loved anyone?

Now, that's a cracking question to end with—very good. No, never. [Laughter.] If he had, he couldn't possibly be what he is. You will find out a lot more about that. It is a good question, because it leads us rather neatly to Half Blood Prince, although I repeat for the millionth time that Voldemort is not the half

blood prince, which is what a lot of people thought. He is definitely, definitely not.

Hermione's little brother. "Shermione."

Does Hermione have any brothers or sisters?

No, she doesn't. When I first made up Hermione I gave her a younger sister, but she was very hard to work in. The younger sister was not supposed to go to Hogwarts. She was supposed to remain a Muggle. It was a sideline that didn't work very well and it did not have a big place in the story. I have deliberately kept Hermione's family in the background. You see so much of Ron's family so I thought that I would keep Hermione's family, by contrast, quite ordinary. They are dentists, as you know. They are a bit bemused by their odd daughter but quite proud of her all the same. (Edinburgh Book Festival, 8/15/04, http://www.jkrowling.com/textonly/news_view.cfm?id=80)

Harry's mysterious (and non-existent) godmother.

Does Harry have a godmother? If so, will she make an appearance in future books?

No, he doesn't. I have thought this through. If Sirius had married... Sirius was too busy being a big rebel to get married. When Harry was born, it was at the very height of Voldemort fever last time so his christening was a very hurried, quiet affair with just Sirius, just the best friend. At that point it looked as if the Potters would have to go into hiding so obviously they could not do the big christening thing and invite lots of people. Sirius is the only one, unfortunately. I have got to be careful what I say there, haven't I? (Edinburgh Book Festival, 8/15/04, http://www.jkrowling.com/textonly/news_view.cfm?id=80).

Voldemort called "Voldie," or morphing into a good guy.

I would like to take this opportunity to say that the practise of calling Lord Voldemort 'Voldie' must stop, as must the insistence that with a bit of therapy 'Voldie' would be a real sweetheart. (jkrowling.com, http://www.jkrowling.com/textonly/news_view.cfm?id=63)

Voldemort in Tom Riddle's 16-year-old body from Chamber of Secrets.

> In 'Chamber of Secrets', what would have happened if Ginny had died and Tom Riddle had escaped the diary?

> I can't answer that fully until all seven books are finished, but it would have strengthened the present-day Voldemort considerably. (jkrowling.com, http://www.jkrowling.com/textonly/faq_view.cfm?id=17)

"Icicle," or "Professor Bicycle."

> I have been told that I once promised a character with this name during an interview. I can only think that somebody misheard what I said because at no stage have I ever planned a character called 'Icicle.'

> Professor Bicycle, on the other hand, will be a key figure in books six and seven.*

> *this is a joke (jkrowling.com, http://www.jkrowling.com/textonly/rumours_view.cfm?id=1)

J.K. Rowling's patented mystery-erasing device.

> You would all like me to tell you exactly what happens in books six and seven and then to erase your memories so that you can read them. I know, because that is how I feel about things that I really enjoy. I would kind of like to do it, but at the same time I know that I would ruin it for everyone. (Edinburgh Book Festival, 8/15/04, http://www.jkrowling.com/textonly/news_view.cfm?id=80). ✗

Things we may see in books six or seven

The door has been left open on a few intriguing items. More will be added to this list in subsequent editions!

Ron & Hermione together

Will Ron and Hermione ever get together?

Well—[Laughter.] What do you think? [Audience member: I think they will]. I'm not going to say. I can't say, can I? I think that, by now, I've given quite a lot of clues on the subject. That is all I'm going to say. You will have to read between the lines on that one. (Edinburgh Book Festival, 8/15/04, http://www.jkrowling.com/textonly/news_view.cfm?id=80).

Part Three: Harry Potter book seven

Finally ... book seven!

After "Harry Potter and the Half-Blood Prince" will come Harry Potter book seven, the culmination of the series.

- No one knows yet what the title will be—but there is a set of plausible candidates.

- No one knows yet when the book will come out—but it will probably be within a year or two of publication of HBP.

- No-one knows everything that the book will contain—but J. K. Rowling has dropped a lot of hints over the years about what will, won't, and may be found in book seven.

J. K. Rowling and her publisher have trademarked these titles

Someone called "Prez_Shadowfax" was prescient enough to do a trademark search with the United Kingdom Patent Office (http://www.patent.gov.uk) on December 28, 2003 and he found some fascinating stuff (http://www.livejournal.com/users/prez_shadowfax/?skip=20).

> Guess what I found? I think this is a list of potential titles for the next two books...I'll list them here[.] The ones in **bold** are new applications - made on the 24/7/2003, which is after the Order of the Phoenix was released. ...I tell you, this is BIG BIG NEWS!!! *jumps up and down in delight*
>
> -Harry Potter and the Alchemist's Cell
>
> **-Harry Potter and the Battle for Hogwarts**
>
> -Harry Potter and the Chariots of Light
>
> **-Harry Potter and the Final Revelation**
>
> **-Harry Potter and the Great Revelation**

-Harry Potter and the Green Flame Torch

Forget about this one, per the author herself, as noted in Part One.

this green torch business seems to be cropping up everywhere. Do you really think getting rid of Voldemort would be that easy? (jkrowling.com, http://www.jkrowling.com/textonly/rumours_view.cfm?id=10)

-Harry Potter and the Half-Blood Prince

Forget about this one—it's already taken!

-Harry Potter and the Hallows of Hogwarts

-Harry Potter and the Hogsmeade Tomb

-Harry Potter and the Hogwarts Hallows

-Harry Potter and the Mudblood Revolt

-Harry Potter and the Parseltongue Trophy

-Harry Potter and the Pyramids of Furmat

-Harry Potter and the Quest of the Centaur

-Harry Potter and the Realm of the Lion

-Harry Potter and the Serpent's Revenge

-Harry Potter and the Shadow of the Serpent

An updated search carried out in September 2004 found the following new trademarks that were filed in June 2004.

Harry Potter And The Curse Of The Dementors

Harry Potter And The Death's Head Plot

Harry Potter And The Serpent Prince

Harry Potter And The Tower Of Shadows

These last two are not likely, as they are too similar to a set of titles explicitly ruled out by J. K. Rowling:

The SpongeBob connection: All the trademark applications listed above were filed by a company called "Seabottom Productions Ltd."

[Rumour:] Book six is going to be called 'Harry Potter and the Green Flame Torch' or 'the Mountain of Fantasy' and book seven is going to be called 'Harry Potter and the Fortress of Shadows' or 'the Forest of Shadows'

Not even close! Who makes these up?! (jkrowling.com, http://www.jkrowling.com/textonly/rumours_view.cfm?id=10)

And oddly enough, all four of the June 2004 applications were withdrawn. The obvious reason is that the publisher decided they were no longer needed... but why?

Eliminating the ruled out or withdrawn candidates leaves us with

Harry Potter and the Alchemist's Cell

Harry Potter and the Battle for Hogwarts

Harry Potter and the Chariots of Light

Harry Potter and the Final Revelation

Harry Potter and the Great Revelation

Harry Potter and the Hallows of Hogwarts

Harry Potter and the Hogsmeade Tomb

Harry Potter and the Hogwarts Hallows

Harry Potter and the Mudblood Revolt

Harry Potter and the Parseltongue Trophy

Harry Potter and the Pyramids of Furmat

Harry Potter and the Quest of the Centaur

Harry Potter and the Realm of the Lion

Harry Potter and the Serpent's Revenge

Harry Potter and the Shadow of the Serpent

Out of all these, my favorite is "Harry Potter and the Battle for Hogwarts," simply because the whole series has been about Hogwarts.

When will we find out the real title of book seven?

Don't expect to find out the real title until well after the release of "Harry Potter and the Half-Blood Prince." At the Edinburgh Book Fair in August 2004, Rowling said:

"I'm not going to tell you, I'm sorry. The trouble I would be in if I did. My agent would have me hunted down." (Sunday Times, 8/20/04)

This *is* a bit of a puzzler. She's the *autho*r, after all?. Why *can't* she reveal the title?

My best guess is that the publishers and movie companies are concerned about protecting their intellectual property. There would be an immediate rush to hijack domain names and trademarks. So Rowling is under pressure to make sure everyone else has time to do their jobs properly.

How long will book seven be?

Chances are that it will be shorter than "Order of the Phoenix," the heavyweight champ of the series, as Rowling has said she does not want to keep churning out "baby hippos." (jkrowling.com, http://www.jkrowling.com/textonly/faq_view.cfm?id=35) My own guess is that it will be quite a bit shorter, more like the length of "Chamber of Secrets" or "Azkaban." Rowling knows what has to be in book seven, and she will take as much space as it needs, no more, no less. ✄

Things we will definitely see in book seven

J. K. Rowling has made a number of definite statements about exactly what will be found in book seven. The following list of quotations summarizes her commitments.

What happens to everyone.

> The final chapter for Book Seven is written. I wrote that just for my own satisfaction, really as an act of faith. (To say) I will get here in the end. In that chapter you do, I hope, feel a sense of resolution. You do find out what happens to the survivors. I know that sounds very ominous (laughs). (The Oregonian,10/20/00, http://www.quick-quote-quill.org/articles/2000/1000-oregonian-baker.htm).

More about the scar.

> In plotting Harry's journey she has already completed a draft of the final chapter of the last book. "I constantly rewrite," she says. "At the moment, the last word is 'scar.'" (People Magazine, 12/31/99, reproduced at http://www.quick-quote-quill.org/articles/1999/1299-people.html).

Something "incredibly important" about Harry Potter's mother.

> Now, the - the important thing about Harry's mother - the really, really significant thing - you're going to find out in two - in two parts. You'll find out a lot more about her in book five, or you'll find out something very significant about her in book five, and you'll find out something incredibly important about her in book seven. . ("The Connection" radio show, 10/12/99, http://www.hogwarts-library.net/reference/interviews/19991012_TheConnection.txt).

The explanation of why James Potter died before Lily Potter.

> At the end of 'Goblet of Fire', in which order should Harry's parents have come out of the wand?

> Lily first, then James. That's how it appears in my original manuscript but we were under enormous pressure to edit it very fast and my American editor thought that was the wrong way around, and he is so good at catching small errors I changed it without thinking, then realised it had been right in the first place. We were all very sleep-deprived at the time.

How Harry Potter will become

> "a full wizard, and free to use his magic outside school." (Barnesandnoble.com online chat, 3/19/99, http://search.barnesandnoble.com/booksearch/isbninquiry.asp?ean=9780590353427&displayonly=ITV#ITV).

Something "stunning" (and probably not good) about Professor Snape.

> Lydon: Er - one of our connec- one of our internet correspondents wondered if Snape is going to fall in love?
>
> JKR: Yeah? Who on earth would want Snape in love with them, that is a very horrible idea. Erm ...
>
> Lydon: But you'd get an important kind of redemptive pattern to Snape
>
> JKR: It is, isn't it ... I got ... There's so much I wish I could say to you, and I can't because it'd ruin ... I promise you ... whoever asked that question, can I just say to you that I'm - I'm slightly stunned that you've said that - erm - and you'll find out why I'm so stunned if you read book 7. ("The Connection" radio show, 10/12/99, http://www.hogwarts-library.net/reference/interviews/19991012_TheConnection.txt).

When I re-read the series after seeing this comment, I noticed something ... if you read what J. K. Rowling actually writes, Snape never does anything nice. Ever. The idea that he's a good guy underneath it all comes strictly from our imaginations.

One of Harry's classmates ends up as a teacher at Hogwarts.

> JKR: Erm, well, because all your kids said hello so nicely in the background there, I'm going to give you information I haven't given anyone else, and I will tell you that one of the characters - er - one of - one of Harry's class mates, though it's not Harry himself, does end up a teacher at Hogwarts, but _it_is_not_maybe_the_one_you'd_think_ - hint, hint, hint! So, yes one of them does end up staying at Hogwarts, but - erm ...
>
> Lydon: Does the kids want to have a guess at it, Kathleen?
>
> Kathleen: Do you like to have a guess at who it is?
>
> Class: Ron
>
> Kathleen: They say Ron ...
>
> JKR: Noooo - it's not Ron ...
>
> Kathleen: [to class] it's not Ron ...
>
> JKR: ... because I can't see Ron as a teacher, no way. ("The Connection" radio show, 10/12/99, http://www.hogwarts-library.net/reference/interviews/19991012_TheConnection.txt [(My money's on Neville Longbottom.)

What makes some witches and wizards become ghosts after they die, and some not.

> You don't really find that out until Book VII, but I can say that the happiest people do not become ghosts. As you might guess, Moaning Myrtle! (Scholastic live interview, 2/3/00, http://www.scholastic.com/harrypotter/author/transcript1.htm

A neat ending. There will not be a lot of loose ends.

> P: Are you going to have a lot of loose ends to tie up in 7?

> JKR: Oh god, I hope not. I'm aiming to tie it all up neatly in a nice big knot... that's it, good night. (CBC Newsround, 6/19/03, http://news.bbc.co.uk/cbbcnews/hi/uk/newsid_3004000/3004878.stm)

Things we will definitely NOT see in book seven

We will not see anyone who is definitely dead come back to life. This specifically includes Harry's mother.

> Lydon: Peter, what is your guess about Lily - the real story about Harry's mother?

> Peter: Er - I don't really know, but I'm guessing that maybe she is going to come back to life, maybe in the seventh book or something like that ...

> JKR: Well, it would be nice, but - I'll tell you something - you - you've raised a really interesting point there, Peter, because when I started writing the books, the first thing I had to decide was not what magic /can/ do, but what it /can't/ do. I had to set limits on it - immediately, and decide what the parameters are ... and one of the most important things I - I decided was that _magic__cannot__bring__dead__people__back to life; that' - that's one of the most profound things, the - the natural law of - of - of death applies to wizards as it applies to Muggles and there is no returning once you're properly dead, you know, they might be able to save very close-to-death people better than we can, by magic - that they - that they have certain knowledge we don't, but once you're dead, you're dead.

> So - erm - yeah, I'm afraid there will be no coming back- for Harry's parents.

Harry as Minister of Magic.

> Seventeen is much too young to enter politics. (jkrowling.com, http://www.jkrowling.com/textonly/rumours_view.cfm?id=12)

Nor will Arthur Weasley be the new Minister for Magic.

> "Alas, no." (jkrowling.com, http://www.jkrowling.com/textonly/faq_view.cfm?id=59)

Things we MAY learn in book seven

More about the moral and religious implications of the books.

> Rowling, aware of the protest, said she couldn't answer the questions about the book's religious content until the conclusion of book seven. (Chicago Sun-Times, 10/22/99, http://www.quick-quote-quill.org/articles/1999/1099-chictimes-tucker.html).

Whether Voldemort will be invincible?

> pablo: If Harry dies in the ending of the books, will Voldemort be invincible?

> JK Rowling replies -> Pablo, I can't possibly answer. You'll have to read book seven! (World Book Day Chat, 3/04/04, http://www.mugglenet.com/jkrwbd.shtml)

Someone in a good position to wonder has a bad feeling about it ...

> Daniel Radcliffe, who plays Harry Potter in the movie versions of the books, admitted on the set of the forthcoming Goblet of Fire film that he fears Voldemort can only be killed if the boy wizard dies too. (Toronto Sun, 9/5/04).

Whether Harry will ever graduate from Hogwarts.

> But when she was asked if Harry would ever get to wear Hogwarts graduation robes, she said: 'It would give quite a lot away if I answered that, so I am not going to.' (Scottish Daily, 7/9/04)

Things we will not find out until book seven

The final revelation:

> josh from Cottenham Village College: Right at the beginning, when Voldemort tried to kill Harry, how did Voldemort and Harry both survive? *Schools Competition Winner*

> JK Rowling replies -> That is the crucial and central question and if I answered it there would be hardly any point writing books six and seven... so I won't!

Part Four: book eight and beyond

There may be a revised edition of the entire series

In a World Book Day chat in April 2004, Rowling appeared pretty interested in doing a revised edition of the series—let's call it Harry Potter version 1.1.

> Tanya J Potter: If you could change anything about Harry Potter what would it be?

> JK Rowling replies -> There are loads of things I would change. I don't think any writer is ever completely happy with what they've written. One of these days - once seven is finished - I'll revise all seven books (World Book Day Chat, 3/04/04, http://www.mugglenet.com/jkrwbd.shtml).

Although this sounds pretty positive, my gut feeling is that she won't do this revision for a while. The reason is simple: it will be a lot of work for her, and not terribly interesting work at that. She's a creative person, and she will want to spend her time and energy on writing new stuff!

On the other hand, this talk of a revised version is great news for her publishers. Once she revises the series, they can sell seven *more* books to each of her fans. It is also great news for Harry Potter fandom, since it means there will be two versions of the "canon" to argue over, and any theory can always be supported by a reference to an alternate version of the story. ✔

We will not see "Harry Potter: Episode One"

George Lucas has made three very expensive and critically disliked "prequels" to his "Star Wars" series. J. K. Rowling does not want to follow in his footsteps.

> Will there be a book about Harry's Mum and Dad, about how they became friends and how they died?

> So it would be "Harry Potter: Episode One". [Laughter]. No, but a lot of people have asked that. It is all George Lucas's fault. You won't need a prequel; by the time I am finished, you will know enough. I think it would be shamelessly exploitative to do that. I am sure that Mr Lucas is doing it only for artistic reasons, but in my case I think that by the time you have had the seven books you will know everything you need to know for the story. (Edinburgh Book Festival, 8/15/04).

And confirmed on the website:

> Hmm... once again, too much Star Wars can do this to a person. No prequels are planned. (jkrowling.com, http://www.jkrowling.com/textonly/rumours_view.cfm?id=6) ✗

Harry Potter book eight: an encyclopedia?

Although there won't be an eighth novel, there may very well be an eighth *book* in the Harry Potter series, according to J. K. Rowling.

> She said: "I'm not going to say I'll never write anything to do with the world of Hogwarts ever again. Because I have often thought that (if I wrote) book eight, I think it would be right and proper that it should be a book whose royalties go to charity entirely."

> "It could be the encyclopaedia of the world (of Hogwarts) and then I could rid myself of every last lurking details, but no not a novel." (Ananova, 12/01, http://www.quick-quote-quill.org/articles/2001/1201-ananova-staff.htm)

The Encylopedia would be similar to her two previous charity books, "Fantastic Beasts and Where to Find Them" and "Quidditch Through the Ages" – but probably much longer!

The Encyclopedia will certainly include lots of good stuff on the students at Hogwarts.

> She has [a]booklet of every pupil. Their parentage in terms of allegiances to dark forces. Their magical ability. Every character is there in alphabetical order. (J. K. Rowling, Harry Potter and Me Special, 12/28/01, http://www.mugglenet.com/jkrshow.shtml)

There will be more about dementors, but not 150 pages worth.

> Kirk Wilkins: Will you ever publish all your notebooks of information on the series? I am very interested in reading 150 pages on the history of the dementors!
> JK Rowling replies -> lol! Who said there were 150 pages on the dementors??? I certainly didn't! I don't think I'll ever publish my notebooks. Too many revealing doodlings! (World Book Day chat, 3/04/04, http://www.mugglenet.com/jkrwbd.shtml)

It's interesting that she is perfectly willing to talk about publishing an encyclopedia, but not her notebooks. What could she be hiding? Ok, it could be just personal stuff … "I heart Harry" … but maybe there's more to it than that! Some tantalizing details about Harry Potter may have to wait until Rowling's death, or beyond.

J. K. Rowling used "Fantastic Beasts" and "Quidditch" to bury some potentially important facts, like the fact that Hermione's companion, Crookshanks, is not just an ordinary cat. Watch for the Harry Potter encyclopedia to include a few buried nuggets that cast a new light on the events of the series. Also expect Rowling to use the encyclopedia to correct persistent misunderstandings of her work—for example, don't expect the entry on "Draco Malfoy" to make him sound like a good boy to marry! ✗

What else can we expect from J. K. Rowling??

We can expect J. K. Rowling to keep writing creatively! It seems to be something that she needs to do. She's already dreading the end of the series.

> I'll just keep writing. I'll probably just start a completely new plot in book seven. It's going to be very difficult to leave it. I mean, I do look forward to a post-Harry era in my life, because some of the things that go along with this are not that much fun, but at the same time, I dread leaving Harry... because I've been working on it over what I sincerely hope will prove to have been the most turbulent part of my life and that was the constant, and I worked on it so hard for so long - then it will be over and I think it's going to leave a massive gap. (BBC, 6/19/03; http://news.bbc.co.uk/1/hi/entertainment/arts/3004456.stm)

That's a tantalizing hint there about "starting a new plot" in the middle of book seven. Is it possible that she will return to the world of Muggles and witches, but without Harry Potter? The answer to that may depend on the outcome of book seven.

It sounds as if she is still feeling creative.

> JP: Do you know what you will go on to next after that?
>
> JKR: Well, while I was in between, during the three years I've just had [between GoF and OOtP], I was writing something else for a while which was really great, it was good, and I might go back to that. I don't know.
>
> JP: Is that an adult novel?
>
> JKR: Mmmm. It's just something completely different. It was very liberating to do it. (CBBC Newsround, 6/19/03, http://news.bbc.co.uk/cbbcnews/hi/uk/newsid_3004000/3004878.stm).

The problem she faces is that her second act will be under incredible scrutiny.

> JP: Be quite difficult for you though. You'd have to publish under a pseudonym wouldn't you?
>
> JKR: Exactly. But they'll find out within seconds. I don't underestimate the investigative powers of the press, but I don't know what I'll do. (CBBC Newsround, 6/19/03, http://news.bbc.co.uk/cbbcnews/hi/uk/newsid_3004000/3004878.stm).

Expect her to write, and to be published.

> I mean, I know I will definitely still be writing. Will I publish? I don't know. It's what you said, of course you write to be published, because you write to share the story. (CBBC Newsround, 6/19/03, http://news.bbc.co.uk/cbbcnews/hi/uk/newsid_3004000/3004878.stm).

Just be ready for some whining by critics and even by fans.

> But I do think back to what happened to AA Milne, and he of course tried to write adult novels, and was never reviewed without the mention of Tigger, Pooh and Piglet. And I would imagine that the same will happen with me. And that's fine. God knows my shoulders are broad enough, I could cope with that. (CBBC Newsround, 6/19/03,
> http://news.bbc.co.uk/cbbcnews/hi/uk/newsid_3004000/3004878.stm).

And for a possibly maddening delay!

> … I would like some time to have some normal life at the end of the series, and probably the best way to get that isn't to publish immediately. (CBBC Newsround, 6/19/03,
> http://news.bbc.co.uk/cbbcnews/hi/uk/newsid_3004000/3004878.stm).

Last but not least, we can expect J. K. Rowling to continue as a strong advocate for good in the world. The Sunday Times (South Africa) reported this great item in late summer 2004:

> "After reading a recent report that six mentally handicapped children had been discovered in cages in a Prague mental institution, Rowling wrote a fearsome letter to the Czech ambassador in the UK, saying she was "horrified beyond words. The very idea of being locked in a cage around the clock is enough to give adults nightmares."

> Just a day after it had been handed to that country's president, he ordered the removal of caged beds for both adults and children in all psychiatric facilities. It's not only on Earth, then, that JK Rowling is storing up her riches." (Sunday Times [South Africa], 8/23/2004). [Well said!—wfz] ✔

Part Five: while you wait

Wait, wait, wait ...

As a devoted Harry Potter fan, you have several waiting periods ahead of you. First, the wait for "Harry Potter and the Half-Blood Prince" (we discussed the timeline for the book in Part One). Then, perhaps even more agonizing, the wait for Harry Potter Book Seven—most likely, another year or two after the release of HBP. And it's not over then ... because there's still the wait for the movie version of "Harry Potter and the Half-Blood Prince" (November 2008, according to the Internet Movie Database) and the movie version of Harry Potter Book Seven (November 2009?), not to mention waiting for the full DVD set with extended and deleted scenes (spring 2010?), followed by the definitive Harry Potter revised edition, the Harry Potter encyclopedia, and Unknown J. K. Rowling Title #1 (see Part Four for more about these last three items). That's a lot of waiting! What to do while you wait? Well, there's one option that makes a lot of sense, although it isn't very much fun.

Wait!

Here's one super-mature way of dealing with the suspense on book six: wait until book seven comes out and then buy them both! Jan van Aalderen of the Netherlands expressed this point of view nicely:

> That's why the wise thing to do is not buy any book of a series until the series is complete. A rule against which I may sin now and than - like with HP--, but which usually saves me lots of money because not only will I be buying series of books that are no longer in fashion and therefore at a very low price, but also because I will not buy series that are discontinued or otherwise incomplete.. (alt.fan.harry-potter, 7/31/04)

If this recommendation fails to thrill, you do have options.

Look for more info

You can always look for more information about what's coming next. As always, the most authoritative source of information is J. K. Rowling herself. You can start by familiarizing yourself with what she has already said.

<u>Start with the jkrowling.com web site</u>

J. K. Rowling's web site, at http://www.jkrowling.com, sets a great example for popular authors by providing authentic, detailed information straight from the horse's mouth. There are two main versions of the web site: the color "flash" version, and text-only.

- Naturally, the color version looks a lot better, and has a lot more of the flavor of J. K. Rowling.

- The text version has only two advantages, but they are important ones: it is faster, and it will work with any browser.

The site is divided into nine major sections:

- Welcome
- News
- Rumours
- F.A.Q.
- Fan Sites
- Biography
- Extra Stuff
- Wizard of the Month
- Links

It will be well worth your while to read every article on the site. It's particularly worthwhile to check back on the "News", "Rumours," and "Links" pages.

Find the Easter Eggs at jkrowling.com

> A few months ago, J.K. Rowling -- the author of the Harry Potter books -- reinvented her website, and it's become a very popular one, too, among Potter fans. (There are a few of them out there, you know). The design is clever: it's modelled on her actual desktop and offers plenty to poke out, including some hidden surprises. You could put your ingenuity to work in uncovering them, or you could be a lazy Muggle like me, and type "Easter eggs" (what these sorts of things are often called) and the site address into a search engine, and then take it from there. (David Gushum, The Telegram, July 2, 2004)

You can also watch Potter news sites, where directions on how to solve new puzzles are usually posted within hours of first release.

Read Rowling interviews and on-line chats

This book does a good job of summarizing them, but you can get even more detail by reading the original chat transcripts. I found several good sources for historical lists of Rowling interviews.

- Madam Scoop http://www.mutabilisdesign.com/harry/ has chronological and thematic listings.

- Quick Quotes http://www.quick-quote-quill.org/ -- includes a search engine – very useful if you want to find everything Rowling's ever said about, say, "dementors."

- Hogwarts Library Interviews http://www.hogwarts-library.net/reference/interviews/ – clean list of several of the major interviews.

You can watch for news about future interviews with J. K. Rowing in several ways. The ideal is to participate in the on-line chat, if you can. The best places to go for news about upcoming chats are:

- Jkrowling.com

- Bloomsbury.com (UK publisher)

- Scholastic.com (US publisher)

You shouldn't need any special software to participate in the chat—just an up-to-date web browser like Internet Explorer 6 or Mozilla Firefox.

If you are happy reading a summary of the chat afterwards, the simplest thing to do is to watch the headlines in your local newspaper and at websites like CNN.com and BBC News (http://news.bbc.co.uk/).   If you watch those places, news about Rowling interviews will eventually reach you. But it may take a few days or even weeks, and you won't get all the details.

If you want to read the actual transcript of a chat that has occurred recently, check the sites listed above.

Surf the web for Potter web sites

There is a great wealth of Harry Potter web sites, so many that I can't possibly do justice to them all. I will simply provide a list of a few favorites here.

> Tip: when you do a search on "Half-Blood Prince", use the quotes, or else you will get a lot of hits about vampires and rock musicians!

- The Akashic Record http://www.m5p.com/~pravn/hp.
- The Dark Mark http://www.darkmark.com/
- Godric's Hollow http://www.godrics-hollow.net/

> A great site run by real enthusiasts. The people who designed this site have really Thought It Through – my kind of people. I am however shocked at the number of moderators who want to be sorted into Slytherin… and you should know that the Hufflepuffs' common room isn't a dungeon, it's more a cellar - a subtle but important difference (jkrowling.com, http://www.jkrowling.com/textonly/fansite_view.cfm?id=2)

- Harry Potter Automatic News Aggregator http://www.hpana.org
- Harry Potter Facts <http://www.harrypotterfacts.com/
- Harry Potter International http://www.iharrypotter.net/
- Harry Potter Lexicon http://www.hp-lexicon.org/

> This is such a great site that I have been known to sneak into an internet café while out writing and check a fact rather than go into a bookshop and buy a copy of Harry Potter (which is embarrassing). A website for the dangerously obsessive; my natural home. (jkrowling.com, http://www.jkrowling.com/textonly/fansite_view.cfm?id=14)

- Harry Potter's Page http://www.harrypotterspage.com/
- Hogwarts Library <http://www.hogwarts-library.net/
- The Leaky Cauldron http://www.the-leaky-cauldron.org
- MuggleNet http://www.mugglenet.com – J. K. Rowling's site of the month in September 2004.

It's high time I paid homage to the mighty MuggleNet. Where to start? I love the design, (I currently favour the 'Dementor' layout), the polls (I actually voted in the 'Who's the Half-Blood Prince?' one), the pretty-much-exhaustive information on all books and films, the wonderful editorials (more insight there than in several companion volumes I shall not name), 101 Ways to Annoy Lord Voldemort (made me laugh aloud), the Wall of Shame (nearly as funny as some of the stuff I get)... pretty much everything. Webmaster Emerson, Eric, Jamie, Damon, Ben, Matthew, Rachel, Jaymz and Sharon, I salute you. (jkrowling.com)

- Potter verse FAQ http://www.hogwarts-library.net/reference/potterverse_faq.html
- Wizard News http://www.wizardnews.com/: General news, sorted into

Discussion Groups where "Half-Blood Prince" is Discussed

Another fun way to kill time is to participate in on-line discussion groups where "Harry Potter and the Half-Blood Prince" is discussed. There are many options here, I will just offer a few of the obvious ones.

- MuggleNet's Chamber of Secrets discussion forum — http://www.cosforums.com
- The Usenet discussion group alt.fan.harry-potter, available using any newsreader like Outlook Express, or via Google Groups. Warning, Usenet is not moderated and is not 100% child-safe.
- Yahoo! Groups – do a search at http://groups.yahoo.com, or go directly to http://groups.yahoo.com/search?query=%22half-blood%22&submit=Search. There are several HBP lists already.

Where not to go for info

Don't go to Edinburgh to ask J.K. Rowling for details in person. Here is the advice that an article in her home-town newspaper, the Scotsman, gave Edinburghers during the annual Festival:

It may be a solitary, bespectacled American, it could be a gaggle of children, but at some point during the month of August you are likely to be approached by a person or persons anxious to learn the address of Harry Potter author and

Edinburgh institution JK Rowling. There are two ways to handle this delicate situation. The first is to politely explain that unlike our other national treasures, there are no set opening hours at chez Rowling and visitors are unlikely to be given a guided tour and dispatched with an early chapter of Harry Potter and the Half-Blood Prince. The second is to rattle off a complicated sequence of "sharp lefts" and "second rights", safe in the knowledge that these fans are unlikely to find their way back. To you, at least. ⚡

Take the Half-Blood Prince Meme

Take this Half-Blood Prince self-quiz, inspired by the Harry Potter Meme circulating at

http://www.livejournal.com/users/dreamsome/261704.html

- Who's the Half-Blood Prince?

- Is the Half-Blood Prince literally "half-blood", or just $99^{44/100\%}$ magical with that one icky drop of Muggle blood?

- Is the Half-Blood Prince literally a prince?

- If you could have Jar's ear, what would you:
  - Beg her for?
  - Beg her not to do?
  - Expect her to throw you out for mentioning?

- Will Sirius return from the dead?

- Which major character will be the next to die?

- Which character you adore are you afraid will die?

- Which annoying character do you hope will die? ✗

Get Your Own Half-Blood Prince E-mail Address

An enterprising E-Bay auctioneer has signed up for "choice" e-mail addresses like IAmTheHalfBloodPrince@gmail.com, and you can buy them for a low, low $2.99! Check out auctions like the one at http://cgi.ebay.com/ws/eBayISAPI.dll?ViewItem&item=3840364779&category=50 972. ✄

Lurk for "Squidward" while you wait

Keep an eye out for on-line chatters who have a strange fascination with SpongeBob SquarePants.

> A few weeks ago I did something I've never done before and took a stroll into a Harry Potter chat room: specifically, MuggleNet's chat room. ... I might drop in again some time to check that you've done as you've been told. Look out for 'Squidward'. (jkrowling.com, http://www.jkrowling.com/textonly/news_view.cfm?id=63)

Take-back:

> incidentally... I wasn't really Squidward that day in the MuggleNet chat room, either. That's a SpongeBob SquarePants in-joke. I used a different name. So you can all stop logging on as Squidward now ;) (jkrowling.com, http://www.jkrowling.com/textonly/rumours_view.cfm?id=20) ✗

Read while you wait

Who better to recommend some casual reading than J. K. Rowling?

> Are there any books you would recommend to your fans to read while they await Book 5?
>
> JKR: Loads! Read E. Nesbit, Philip Pullman, Henrietta Branford, Paul Gallico. Just read! (Scholastic live interview, 10/16/00, http://www.scholastic.com/harrypotter/author/transcript2.htm).

Certain names, like Pullman and Gallico, come up again and again in Rowling's interviews.

> Excellent question! Read "Clockwork" by Phillip Pullman or "Skellig" by David Almond or... let's see... anything by Paul Gallico, or "The Little White Horse" (for girls!) by Elizabeth Goudge or... ANYTHING! Just keep reading! (AOL interview, 10/19/00, http://www.mugglenet.com/aolchat1.shtml).
>
> When I was a child, I would read absolutely anything. My favourite books for younger people would be I Capture the Castle by Dodie Smith, which I really love, The Little White Horse, all the classic children's books... I love E Nesbit—I think she is great and I identify with the way that she writes. Her children are very real children and she was quite a groundbreaker in her day.

And for adults:

> I also read a lot of adult books. The last novel that I read was Wilkie Collins' The Moonstone, which I have been meaning to read for years. It is a cracking read. I have just been on holiday and, for the first time in five years, I did not take any Iris Murdoch with me, because it is so depressing. I was just about to put one in my case and I thought, "Why do this? Why put yourself through this?", so I didn't bother. I read Wilkie Collins instead and it was a much better experience. *(Edinburgh Book Festival, 8/15/04, http://www.jkrowling.com/textonly/news_view.cfm?id=80).
>
> What is your favourite book ever (not including Harry Potter)?
>
> Let's see... there are loads... probably 'Emma' by Jane Austen... or 'The Van' by Roddy Doyle... there are so many. (BBC, 3/12/01, http://www.mugglenet.com/bbcchat1.shtml).

But don't bother with anything by Jeffrey Archer!

> What's your most hated book of all time?
>
> That I've ever read? It's probably a Jeffrey Archer. I made myself read one to find out whether it was as bad as I thought, and it was. (BBC, 3/12/01, http://www.mugglenet.com/bbcchat1.shtml).

Don't buy signed copies of "Order of the Phoenix"

If you are tempted to get into book collecting while you wait, think twice.

If you or any of your loved ones is thinking of buying a 'signed' Harry Potter book, please be careful. The number of forged signatures has increased greatly over the last few years.

You should be particularly suspicious of signed copies of 'Order of the Phoenix'. I have never done a book signing for 'Phoenix', so signed British copies are very rare, American copies even rarer and other foreign editions (so far) virtually non-existent. Any copy of 'Phoenix' purporting to have been signed at the 'Piccadilly' signing is highly likely to be a fake, for instance.

I sign books for charity and in special circumstances but, as explained in the FAQ section, I can no longer begin to keep up with the demand for signed books. Unfortunately there are unscrupulous people who are only too ready to step into the breach and exploit Harry Potter fans.
(http://www.jkrowling.com/textonly/news_view.cfm?id=64) ✗

Read Fan Fiction

Fan fiction is written by fans about the characters in J. K. Rowling's universe. A quick warning: some fan fiction is not child-safe. Stay aware from anything that is called "slash" or has an adult contenting rating.

A few good web sites are:

- Fictionalley.org

- HarryPotterFanFiction.com

- FanFiction.net

Here are representative summaries from a couple of frantic stories about the "half-blood prince."

> "Harry Potter and the Half Blood Prince": "Who is the mysterious Half Blood Prince? Is it the third year, Po, who seems to have appeared out of nowhere? Is it Crookshanks, who might not be who he pretends to be? Or is it the one that everyone at Hogwarts most suspects? Harry Potter himself!" (Potter, harrypotterfanfiction.com)

> "Shadows of the Light": "A sixth year story, dark and unique. No two consecutive chapters will be written by the same author in the hopes of writing an interesting fix and getting some underrated authors well-deserved publicity. (Bandofwriters, harrypotterfanfiction.com)

You get the idea. This stuff can be fun. ✗

Sing While You Wait

Is there anything jollier to do? Here are a few favorite fan-written songs.

Some Day The Prince Will Come

To the tune of Some Day My Prince Will Come from Disney's Snow White

Some day the Prince will come

Some day we'll learn his name

But till then to our listgroups we'll go

To unleash all our speculative flow

Someone Jo springs on us

Could be a guy we know

Remus with half blood

Godric or even Dud

His royal descent will show.....

Half Blood Prince

A filk by Gail Bohacek to the tune of Two Princes by the Spin Doctors.

Half Blood Prince will be the title

Of the next book, now

And since, since this clue is vital

I'll take a look, now

At the list of all the choices

Of characters, now

Listen to H.P. Fandom's voice as

They weigh factors, now

J.K. gave this information

At her web site, now

"Storgé", it was a fabrication

She didn't write, now

And furthermore, she tells as compensation

In her story, now

Lord Voldemort's not Prince in the narration

Nor is Harry, now

Voldemort, Harry P.

Neither of these two characters are he

I ain't got no idea who it could be

But everybody's got his own little theory

Everybody's got his own little theory

Say maybe the Prince is Colin Creevey

It could be him, now

Or perhaps it's Justin Finch-Fletchley

It could be him, now

Some say the Prince just might be Seamus

It could be him, now

And others like the thought of Remus

They dig Lupin, now

This Prince is a big mystery

What if instead, now

The Prince is ancient history?

Someone who's dead now

Or a figure of speech produced

To cause some doubt, now?

Or he's somebody not introduced

To freak us out, now?

Who is it? We can guess

Rowling mentioned something about CoS.

I ain't got no favorites, I must confess

But you should listen to some other folks obsess

You should listen to some other folks obsess

I heard the Prince may be Lee Jordan

It could be him, now

And some say Mark Evans is our man

It could be him, now

Some think Kingsley will play the part

Is his blood half now?

Others say Gilderoy Lockhart

Don't make me laugh, now

Somewhere I read it's possible

Hagrid's the one, now

Can not forget Thomas Riddle

The list's not done, now

Roger Davies has been mentioned

And Kirke, Andrew, now

Neville has caught some attention

Dean Thomas too, now

Say maybe the Prince is Colin Creevey

It could be him, now

Or perhaps it's Justin Finch-Fletchley

It could be him, now

Some say the Prince just might be Seamus

It could be him, now

Others like the idea of Remus

They dig Lupin, now

Oh, Rowling!

Who could it be, now?

Oh!

Who, who could it be, now?

Oh, we're in a fix

Who could it be, now?

Come on, who is the Prince who's in Book Six?

Who could it be, now?

Come on, come on, come on

Who could it be, now?

Time will go slow, now

I want to know now!

Who Is The Half Blood Prince?

A filk by Jason LeBouef to the tune of Who Wrote The Book Of Love by The MoM-O-tones aka The Monotones.

I wonder wonder who

ooh who…

Who is the half blood prince?

Tell me, tell me, tell me

Oh who is the half blood prince

Cause Mugglenet and Hogshead

Ain't been quite the same place since

I wonder wonder who

Bee-doo-doo who…

Who is the half blood prince?

I am getting impatient

JK, we wait on you

Cause we gotta know this half blood prince

Find out if it's true

I wonder wonder who

Bee-doo-doo who…

Who is the half blood prince?

Someone said that it's Dudley

I hope it's not that lil' fart

Someone said Tom Riddle

It never never never never never be Voldemort

Someone said it's Sev'rus

With grayed out underpants

And someone said it's Lupin

Won't you give the werewolf a chance

Oh I wonder wonder who

Bee-doo-doo who…

Who is the half blood prince?

JK, JK, JK It all depends on you Cause you said we'll have a half blood prince Will you tell us who?

Oh I wonder wonder who

Bee-doo-doo who…

Who is the half blood prince?

Someone said it's Mark Evans

But he got put on the shelf

Someone said it's Dobby

It never never never never never be a house elf

Someone said Stan Shunpike

But let me say one thing

For me, I think it's Ronnie

Because Weasley Is Our King

Oh I wonder wonder who

Bee-doo-doo who…

Who is the half blood prince?

JK, JK, JK

It all depends on you

Cause you said we'll have a half blood prince

Will you tell us who?

I wonder wonder who

Bee-doo-doo who…

Who is the half blood prince?

I wonder who…

Yeah…

Who is the half blood prince?

50 Ways to Wait for Book 6

A filk by Constance Vigilance to Fifty Ways to Leave Your Lover by Paul Simon

"The writing for Book Six is going well", so says her site.

She's writing every day and sometimes well into the night.

JKR suggests that there are ways to ease our plight

There must be fifty ways to wait for Book Six.

She said it's really not my habit to intrude

Furthermore, I hope this won't be cause for being sued

But until the Harry Potter reading frenzy is renewed

There must be fifty ways to wait for Book Six.

Fifty ways to wait for Book Six

Take off some weight, Kate

Read a fan-fic, Dick

Go back to school, Jewel

Just get a real life

Learn how to knit, Kit

You don't need to admit it

Just start something new, Doo

And please get a life.

Ooo, take off some weight, Kate

Read a fan-fic, Dick

Go back to school, Jewel

Just get a real life

Learn how to knit, Kit

You don't need to admit it

Just start something new, Doo

And please get a life.

She peppered up her website just to drive us all insane

We caught the fly, unlocked the box, and clicked the door in vain

We posted to our scrapbooks everything they can contain

But those fifty ways

She said if you need more, there's a new movie out tonight

And this guy Caurón has finally got the details right

But I can say to you and I don't try to be contrite

There must be fifty ways to wait for Book 6

Fifty ways to wait for Book 6

Take off some weight, Kate

Read a fan-fic, Dick

Go back to school, Jewel

Just get a real life

Learn how to knit, Kit

You don't need to admit it

Just start something new, Doo

And please get a life.

Ooo, take off some weight, Kate

Read a fan-fic, Dick

Go back to school, Jewel

Just get a real life

Learn how to knit, Kit

You don't need to admit it

Just start something new, Doo

And please get a life.

Until the release of "Harry Potter and the Half-Blood Prince"! ✗

Appendix A: J. K. Rowling Interviews

Note: this list contains only on-line interviews that contain information relevant in some way to the topics covered in this book, namely:

- Book six, "Harry Potter and the Half-Blood Prince"
- Books six and seven together
- Book seven
- Book eight and beyond
- What to do while you wait

Edinburgh Book Festival, 8/15/04, http://www.jkrowling.com/textonly/news_view.cfm?id=80

World Book Day chat, 3/04/04, at MuggleNet, http://www.mugglenet.com/jkrwbd.shtml; at the Leaky Cauldron, http://www.the-leaky-cauldron.org/JKRWorldBookDay2004.html; at Wizard News, http://www.wizardnews.com/story.200403042.html

MSN UK, 6/26/03, http://www.msn.co.uk/liveevents/harrypotter/transcript/Default.asp?Ath=f

BBC News, 6/19/03, http://news.bbc.co.uk/1/hi/entertainment/arts/3004456.stm

CBC Newsround, 6/19/03, http://news.bbc.co.uk/cbbcnews/hi/uk/newsid_3004000/3004878.stm

April 11, 2003 CoS DVD Interview with Steve Kloves too

J. K. Rowling, Harry Potter and Me Special, 12/28/01, http://www.mugglenet.com/jkrshow.shtml

Ananova, 12/01, http://www.quick-quote-quill.org/articles/2001/1201-ananova-staff.htm

Cinescape, 11/16/00, http://www.cinescape.com/0/editorial.asp?aff_id=0&jump=next&obj_id=26474&this_cat=Books).

October 20, 2000 Larry King Live

http://www.scholastic.com/harrypotter/author/transcript2.htm

Scholastic live interview, 2/3/00,
http://www.scholastic.com/harrypotter/author/transcript1.htm

People Magazine, 12/31/99, reproduced at http://www.quick-quote-quill.org/articles/1999/1299-people.html

National Press Club Luncheon, 10/20/99, http://www.hogwarts-library.net/reference/interviews/19991020_NPCLuncheon.html

The Oregonian,10/20/00, http://www.quick-quote-quill.org/articles/2000/1000-oregonian-baker.htm).

("The Connection" radio show, 10/12/99, http://www.hogwarts-library.net/reference/interviews/19991012_TheConnection.txt

Barnesandnoble.com online chat, 3/19/99,
http://search.barnesandnoble.com/booksearch/isbninquiry.asp?ean=9780590353427&displayonly=ITV#ITV)

Appendix B: AFHP FAQ

This is the "Frequently Asked Questions" file from the Usenet (unmoderated) newsgroup alt.fan.harry-potter. It covers issues relating to all seven books in the series.

From: Petrea Mitchell

Newsgroups: alt.fan.harry-potter

Subject: FAQ: alt.fan.harry-potter Frequently Asked Questions

Date: Mon, 23 Aug 2004 04:06:41

This is not the official FAQ for alt.fan.harry-potter, because there is no one true official FAQ. There are other FAQs, which can be found at http://www.hogwarts-library.net/reference/ . Of all the general FAQs, this can only claim to be the wordiest.

An HTML version of this FAQ is available at http://www.m5p.com/~pravn/hp/faq.html . The absolute final official archived version is at <archive URL to be added when I can confirm it>.

1. THE NEWSGROUP

1.1 How does this thing work?

Go to the following URL and check out the "What is Usenet" and "Usenet Netiquette" sections: http://www.faqs.org/usenet/usenet.html.

1.2 What's on topic for this group?

Just about anything relating to the Harry Potter books, movies, or merchandise, or to J. K. Rowling. Fan fiction, and detailed discussion thereof, should go to alt.fan.harry-potter.creative.

1.3 What do these abbreviations mean?

a.f.h-p, afh-p, afhp, AFH-P, AFHP - alt.fan.harry-potter

AK - Avada Kedavra

CoS, COS - Harry Potter and the Chamber of Secrets

D - Dumbledore

DA – Dumbledore's Army

DADA - Defense Against the Dark Arts

DE - Death Eater(s)

GoF, GOF - Harry Potter and the Goblet of Fire

HBP - Harry Potter and the Half Blood Prince

JKR - J. K. Rowling

LV - Lord Voldemort

MoM, MOM - Ministry of Magic

MWP&P, MWPP - Messrs. Moony, Wormtail, Padfoot and Prongs

OotP, OOTP, OoP, OOP - Harry Potter and the Order of the Phoenix

PoA, POA - Harry Potter and the Prisoner of Azkaban

PS - Harry Potter and the Philosopher's Stone

SS - Harry Potter and the Sorcerer's Stone

V - Voldemort

1.4 What's a "spoiler"?

In the broadest sense, any information from a book or movie someone hasn't seen yet. For instance, if you haven't read "Harry Potter and the Chamber of Secrets" or seen the movie yet, an explanation of what the Chamber of Secrets is would be a spoiler for you.

Articles which contain important spoilers should precede them with a warning— be sure to mention which book the spoilers are from-- and lines of "spoiler space" so that a reader does not see any spoilers in the first screen of the article. This gives them the chance to skip to the next article to avoid being spoiled. You can put just about anything you want in the lines of spoiler space, although it will help out the blind readers, who have to use text-to-voice translators, if you don't use a bunch of random punctuation.

1.5 What needs to be protected with spoiler space?

One category absolutely needs spoiler space: *any* plot information about an as-yet-unreleased book or movie. Other than that, it's a judgment call. The more significant the information is to the main plot arc, the bigger a surprise it is, the later a book it comes from, the more you should think about putting spoiler space in front of it. Don't expect everyone to have digested all the books, movies, and interviews before starting to read this group.

If you're going to use spoiler space, remember to keep the spoilers out of your subject line, too.

1.6 What's "canon"?

The official version-- any information about the plot, characters, or world of Harry Potter coming from the books or from Rowling herself.

1.7 Do I need to check the Google archive before posting?

Not unless you're posting a hot news tip, in which case the group would appreciate it if you check to make sure you aren't the umpteenth person to tell us about it. Other than that, even if the topic you're raising has been discussed before, you or someone else who has joined this newsgroup in the meantime might have something new to say about it. Reading the rest of this FAQ before you post might be a good idea, though.

1.8 Eek! Is Tom Felton really reading this?

He certainly endorses this newsgroup on his Web site, but he's a busy guy and surely can't keep up with everything here. If your intention in posting is for him to see your message, you would probably do better to use his feedback page: http://thomasfelton.com/feedback.html. I'm sure he'll appreciate your making the effort to contact him directly. So will we.

2. THE BOOKS

2.1 What are the official Harry Potter books?

The main books:

Harry Potter and the Philosopher's Stone (or Sorcerer's Stone, in the US)

Harry Potter and the Chamber of Secrets

Harry Potter and the Prisoner of Azkaban

Harry Potter and the Goblet of Fire

Harry Potter and the Order of the Phoenix

Harry Potter and the Half Blood Prince (upcoming)

Supplementary books:

Fantastic Beasts and Where to Find Them

Quidditch Through the Ages

Anything else is unapproved by Rowling or her publishers, no matter how official it claims to be.

2.2 When will the next book be out?

Next Tuesday. (That's this group's shorthand for "We don't know when.")

The best guess at the moment is that it'll be released in the summer or fall of 2005.

2.3 Why was there such a huge gap between the release of the fourth and fifth books?

The official reasons are the enormous size of the fifth book and a desire to avoid the errors that got into the fourth book when it was rushed out. If you prefer a juicy rumor, pick any or all of the following: marriage, pregnancy, childbirth, writer's block, easy living, and the Stouffer lawsuit.

2.4 Why is it "the Sorcerer's Stone" in the US and "the Philosopher's Stone" everywhere else?

Philosopher's Stone is the proper term. Arthur Levine, the editor handling the US version of the book, wanted to change it because he was concerned that American parents would not understand the reference and would be put off by the academic connotations of "Philosopher". The change was made with Rowling's input and approval. Both Rowling and Levine have expressed regrets since.

2.5 What will book 7 be called?

We don't know yet.

2.6 Where can I download the books?

They do not appear to be available in electronic format.

2.7 No, where can I download illegal copies of them for free?

There are undoubtedly copies circulating out there somewhere, but don't come crying to us when the FBI breaks down your door.

2.8 Will there be an eighth book?

There will be exactly seven books describing Harry's adventures, no more. However, there are already two supplementary books (see 2.1), and Rowling says that she would be willing to do more for charity. She's also raised the possibility of doing a "Hogwarts Encyclopedia" after the whole series has been published, but she is not contractually obligated to do either of these things.

However, one thing she says she will definitely do is revise the whole series once she finishes the seventh book.

2.9 How are the "adult" editions different from the regular ones?

The adult editions have more respectable-looking covers. Not a word of the actual stories is different, but the W. H. Smith "People's Choice" award was given specifically to the adult edition of "Order of the Phoenix."

2.10 What are the differences between the US and UK editions?

The Harry Potter Lexicon maintains lists of differences between the   editions. You can find them from the menu at http://www.hp-lexicon.org/help.html. The differences are mostly due to translating between the dialects (e.g., "jumper" in the UK becomes "sweater" in the US).

3. THE MOVIES

3.1 What can you tell me about the release of the next movie?

The movie adaptation of "Harry Potter and the Goblet of Fire" is expected some time in 2005.

3.2 Will GoF be adapted as one movie or two?

Mike Newell, the director, has been confidently assuring us that it'll be just one.

3.3 Who will be in the upcoming movies?

The adult actors who have appeared in the completed movies are committed to appear in all the movies their characters are in, except for Richard Harris, who discovered the escape clause and was replaced by Michael Gambon. All the child actors are confirmed for GoF; their status for the fifth movie is undetermined but they all sound interested.

New actors announced so far:

Cedric Diggory: Robert Pattinson

Fleur Delacour: Clemence Poesy

Madame Maxime: Frances de la Tour

Mad-Eye Moody: Brendan Gleeson

Rita Skeeter: Miranda Richardson

Voldemort: Ralph Fiennes

No one else is confirmed yet. Please don't believe everything you read in the Internet Movie Database.

3.4 Are the movies canon?

No. The scriptwriter, Steven Kloves, does consult with Rowling, but we have no way of knowing whether information which is not in the books originally came from Rowling or not.

3.5 Where can I download the movies?

Warner Bros. has not made them available for download.

3.6 No, where can I download illegal copies of them for free?

There are undoubtedly copies circulating out there somewhere, but don't come crying to us when the FBI breaks down your door.

4. ELECTRONIC VERSIONS

4.1 How do I get to the deleted scenes on the extras DVD for the first movie?

Settle in, this is a long trip. From the main menu, go to Diagon Alley. Select bricks in any order until you get through the wall. Select the key at the bottom of the sign, then select the stacks of coins. Go back out to Diagon Alley and into Ollivander's. Pick any three wands; the third will be successful. Return to the main menu and go to the classrooms. Select the pedestal by clicking *twice* on it. Select the flute. Select the key with the broken wing (it's the one way in the back). Select the round potion bottle. Select the stone in the mirror and you will at last be at the first deleted scenes menu.

Some people have reported that they can jump to title 80 (completion of the key puzzle) and continue from there to the deleted scenes. Some can't. If you try it and it doesn't work, you will need to restart your DVD entirely to make the long way work.

4.2 Is there another ending to the Chamber of Secrets tour?

No, there's just the one way out.

4.3 Where can I find cheats for the video games?

There are a lot of sites that carry them-- enter "harry potter cheats" and the game platform you are using at your favorite search engine.

5. WEB SITES

5.1 Where are the official sites?

For books, http://www.scholastic.com/harrypotter, and for the movies, http://harrypotter.warnerbros.com/. Be warned that these sites are spectacularly incompatible with anything but the latest popular browsers running with plug-ins and no security.

Rowling's official site is at http://www.jkrowling.com/ and does have a "text version" with more limited information at http://www.jkrowling.com/textonly/.

5.2 Where can I find Harry Potter news?

The Dark Mark http://www.darkmark.com/ : General news.

Godric's Hollow http://www.godrics-hollow.net/ : General news.

Harry Potter International http://www.iharrypotter.net/ : General news.

Harry Potter's Page http://www.harrypotterspage.com/ : General news.

The Leaky Cauldron http://www.the-leaky-cauldron.org/ : Semi- professional news (some official insider access) and activism.

MuggleNet http://www.mugglenet.com : General news.

The Snitch http://www.thesnitch.co.uk/site/ : Primarily movie and merchandise news, but carries major items of general interest.

Wizard News http://www.wizardnews.com/ : General news, sorted into several categories.

Also, Dark Horizons http://www.darkhorizons.com and Counting Down http://www.countingdown.com/, which are general movie news sites, sometimes originate Potter-related news.

5.3 Where can I find fan fiction?

The following is an incomplete list of general Potter fan fiction sites. Left out completely are the countless pages that specialize in particular characters. See your favorite search engine if you want to find one for your favorite character(s).

Fan Domination http://fandomination.net/ (General fanfic site)

FanFic.Net http://www.fanfiction.net/ (General fanfic site)

Fiction Alley http://www.fictionalley.org/

Forever Fandom http://www.foreverfandom.net (General fanfic site)

Harry Potter Fan Fiction http://www.harrypotterfanfiction.com/

Marauders Archive http://fanfiction.bitter-rain.net/

Phoenix Song http://www.phoenixsong.net/

The Sugar Quill http://www.sugarquill.net/

Or, check your favorite news archive for articles on the newsgroup alt.fan.harry-potter.creative.

5.4 What about reference sites?

Harry Potter Lexicon http://www.hp-lexicon.org/ : Complete character information from the books, timelines, explanatory articles, and more.

The Akashic Record http://www.m5p.com/~pravn/hp/ : Basic information from the books, with etymologies, symbolism, and cultural information, organized by spoiler level. (Warning! The author of this FAQ is touting her own site here.)

Harry Potter Facts http://www.harrypotterfacts.com/ : Important facts by chapter, and extensive speculative discussion.

Hogwarts Library http://www.hogwarts-library.net/ : Miscellaneous reference and discussion site organized in support of this newsgroup.

5.5 What's the deal with the door on the Flash side of Rowling's official site?

It opens only sporadically. If it won't open for you, you're not doing anything wrong, it just means she didn't feel like letting it open that day.

6. LEGAL STUFF

6.1 Is my fan site illegal?

It depends on exactly what you have on your site, how you're using it, and whether any of the copyright or trademark holders has asked you to stop. The entertainment industry is aware these days that it is in its best interests to allow online fan communities to flourish, so you're unlikely to get a cease-and-desist letter unless you are doing something like distributing unauthorized copies of the books or movies from your site.

Adding a copyright acknowledgement or a link to an official site isn't going to help you if one of the copyright or trademark holders disapproves of what you're doing. However, if you still would like to include a disclaimer, "SteveD3" reports that when he asked Warner Brothers for official permission for his Web site, they suggested the following:

"HARRY POTTER, HOGWARTS CREST, GRYFFINDOR, RAVENCLAW, HUFFLEPUFF, and SLYTHERIN characters, names and related characters are trademarks of Warner Bros. TM & (C) 2003. Harry Potter Publishing Rights (C) J.K.R. Note the opinions on this site are those made by the owners. All stories (fanfiction) are owned by the author and are not subject to copyright law. This site (C) 2003 ALL RIGHTS RESERVED."

If you are a real stickler for details, change "2003" to the release year of the most recent movie.

6.2 Is fan fiction illegal?

If Rowling or Bloomsbury object to it, yes, but they don't much. Rowling says on her Web site: "Fan fiction is really fun, though, and I am so proud to think that

Harry Potter inspired so much creativity!" On the other hand, she does not approve of adult-oriented fan fiction.

6.3 What's the Stouffer lawsuit about and how is it doing?

Nancy Stouffer, another children's author, accused Rowling of stealing material from her stories to use in the Harry Potter books. Rowling sued to have the accusation disproved, Stouffer made counterclaims, and finally, in September 2002, a judge ruled not only that the similarities between the two authors' works were "minimal and superficial", but that some of Stouffer's evidence was fraudulent, and fined her $50,000. Stouffer appealed the decision, but the appeal was denied in January 2004.

You can read the full text of the original judgment at http://www.eyrie.org/~robotech/stouffer.htm . A report on the appeal is available at http://www.entlawdigest.com/story.cfm?storyID=3094 .

The last section of this FAQ contains MAJOR spoilers! If you haven't read all the books, skip to the next article now!

This space provided to keep you from being inadvertently spoiled by what follows-- this is your last warning!

7. THE RESTRICTED SECTION

7.1 Is there a FAQ which covers the most frequently proposed theories, which you have been dying to tell me about but held back until now because it contains a lot of spoilers?

Yes! Check out the Potterverse FAQ, archived at http://www.hogwarts-library.net/reference/potterverse_faq.html, which also includes answers to a lot of slightly less frequently asked questions that you may want to know.

7.2 Why does James Potter appear before Lily in GoF?

This is an error in the first edition. Since Lily was killed after James, she should appear first, and does in later printings. Part of the reason for the relaxed schedule for the fifth book was to avoid mistakes like this.

7.3 Is Sirius really dead?

Yes. He is no more. He has ceased to be. He is an ex-Sirius.

7.4 Does it say that Voldemort/Tom Riddle dies at the beginning of GoF?

The three Riddles killed at the Riddle house are Tom Riddle *senior*-- Voldemort's Muggle father-- and Tom Riddle Sr.'s mother and father.

7.5 Why couldn't Harry see thestrals before when he'd already been present at his parents' deaths?

Rowling's explanation is that it doesn't count to have seen death unless you understand what you've seen, which wasn't true for Harry until he'd seen Cedric die and had some time to think it over. The carriages were still "horseless" when he was going back to the train station at the end of GoF because it hadn't really sunk in yet.

7.6 How could the Sorting Hat possibly consider putting Harry in Slytherin if he isn't a pureblood?

Salazar Slytherin may have held to the pureblood idea, but it's Godric Gryffindor's hat, and not constrained by that requirement. You may recall that it previously put Tom Riddle Jr., a half-blood, into Slytherin.

7.7 Did Lucius Malfoy really try to AK Harry at the end of CoS??

The book says simply that "he lunged at Harry", so for purposes of canon, probably not. As for the movie, some people hear Malfoy saying "Avada", but some hear "Vada", "Vera", or something along those lines. Closed captioning differs from region to region. The only person who can give us a definitive answer is Jason Isaacs. If you get a chance to ask him about this, please let us know what he says.

7.8 Who are the heads of Hufflepuff and Ravenclaw?

Professor Sprout is the head of Hufflepuff; Professor Flitwick is the head of Ravenclaw.

7.9 What houses were Sirius Black, Remus Lupin, and Peter Pettigrew in?

They were all Gryffindors.

7.10 How did Harry get the Marauder's Map back at the end of GoF?

Rowling said in her 2004 World Book Day online chat that Harry just retrieved it from the fake Moody's office when all the excitement was over.

7.11 What hints has Rowling given us about HBP?

This title was the working title of the second book, but when that book was complete, the story had ended up so different from what she'd planned that the title didn't apply anymore.

The first chapter of this book covers something originally intended for the beginning of PS.

The "Half Blood Prince" is neither Harry nor Voldemort (which also means it isn't Tom Riddle).

Colophon

This book was produced using Microsoft Word and Adobe Acrobat. The cover was produced using The Gimp 2.0.2 with Ghostscript. The cover font is Palatino Linotype. The spine is Verdana.

Heading fonts and the body text inside the book are in Palatino Linotype, chosen because it is a nimble-looking font. Quotations are in Verdana, chosen because it has strong connotations of the Web and the Internet. The end of major sections is signified by the dingbat ⚡ from the Webdings font, chosen because it resembles Harry Potter's lightning bolt scar.

The American Heritage® Dictionary of the English Language, Fourth Edition, copyright © 2000 by Houghton Mifflin Company defines col·o·phon as follows:

> An ancient Greek city of Asia Minor northwest of Ephesus. It was famous for its cavalry.

Along the same lines, Webster's Revised Unabridged, copyright 1996, 1998, MICRA, Inc.:

> \Col"o*phon\ (k[o^]l"[-o]*f[o^]n), n. [L. colophon finishing stroke, Gr. kolofw`n; cf. L. culmen top, collis hill. Cf. Holm.] An inscription, monogram, or cipher, containing the place and date of publication, printer's name, etc., formerly placed on the last page of a book.

J. K. Rowling revealed something about *her* finishing stroke in a 1999 interview with People Magazine.

> "I constantly rewrite," [Rowling] says. "At the moment, the last word is 'scar.'" ⚡